C0 ACB 619

Meditations

Meditations

~⊷◄ *Selections from a* ►⊶~

CENTURY of MOTTOES

Compiled by

ELIZABETH MACLEOD SCATTERGOOD

BENTLEY PRESS
Wayne, Pennsylvania 19087

To my husband Roger,
and to all the members of his remarkable family
whose interest over a hundred years,
has sent forth
the little calendars with great ideas.

1985 by Elizabeth Macleod Scattergood
All rights reserved. This book is protected
by copyright. No part of it may be reproduced
in any manner or by any means without
written permission of the Scattergood family

Library of Congress Catalog Card Number 84-062395
ISBN 0-910702-12-8

PRINTED IN THE UNITED STATES OF AMERICA

Book design by Terry Starr Carrigan

INTRODUCTION

The quotations for *Meditations* were selected from the red, white, and blue "Motto" calendars, familiar to persons of many religious persua-
sions. They were started in in 1884 by Thomas
Scattergood, the Quaker owner of a small manu-
facturing business in Chester, Pennsylvania. The
first issue numbered only fifty copies for the use,
and as he hoped, the profit of the men and boys in
his firm. He thought of the calendars, which every
year he personally prepared, with the assistance of
family members, as his Christian ministry. He dis-
tributed them without cost to offices, schools, and
individuals, as the interest in them grew. He was a
person of great modesty, and preferred that the
calendars not carry his name.

Following the death of Thomas
Scattergood in 1907, the project was continued by
hid son, J. Henry Scattergood. Interested in many
social issues, Henry Scattergood had a special concern for American Indians, and for a time was
Assistant Commissioner of Indian Affairs. The
work on the calendars was shared by his wife,

Ann Theodora. After the latter's death, he was assisted by his second wife, Dorothy. In 1953, Henry Scattergood was no longer able to continue. Elizabeth Scattergood Chalmers, and her husband, A. Burns Chalmers, both affiliated with the American Friends Service Committee, then took on the task, compiling the calendars until 1982. Since then the present editor, with the much appreciated help of her husband, Roger, has been responsible for them.

From a modest beginning of fifty calendars, requests for them increased to a high point in 1966, when a million copies were printed, and sent to all parts of the world. (Since that point, with the appearance on the scene of other fine calendars of quotations, the distribution of the "Motto" calendars has declined to some extent.) Although it was necessary in 1921 to discontinue free distribution, the calendars, since then, have been issued on a low cost basis. Outside of a relatively small circle, the anonymity of the authorship continued until the hundredth year. In consultation with Margaret Scattergood, daughter of the originator, it has been decided that the story of the beginning of the calendars would be an appropriate addition to this anniversary volume.

In making a daily diary of selections from the hundred years of calendars, I have attempted both to give a representative sampling, and at the same time to choose the most thoughtful and substantial quotations. The years from which the quotations are taken are noted on each page.

It is interesting to observe the broadening of focus throughout the century. Perhaps because Thomas Scattergood had his employees as his first consideration, at a time when many employers felt a personal responsibility for their work force, the early calendars had a large number of behavioral admonitions, interspersed with religious precepts. Examples of the former are: "Waste not, want not!" (B. Franklin) "Young man; make your record clean!" (J. Gough) "Live within your income" (Author unknown) "He that buys what he does not want, will soon want what he cannot buy" (Colton) "The way to fare well is to do well" (Unknown) While this type of quotation does not seem appropriate to the purpose of this volume, a number of the religious quotations from the early calendars have been selected.

As the years went on, the editors of the calendars increasingly added to the focus on personal spirituality, an emphasis on the oneness of humankind, as children of God; from this concept emerges the responsibility of the individual to contribute his part in creating a world in which all may live in justice and peace.

Over these hundred years, the deepest thoughts of spiritual men and women from many faiths, many countries, and many centuries have been given to us for our pondering. It is hoped that each reader will find in these pages, something helpful for the journey through the year.

Finally, I wish to thank those who have helped in the preparation of the book: Margaret

Scattergood, for historical data and enthusiastic support; Elizabeth and Burns Chalmers, for helpful information and wise counsel; Bentley Press Limited for their continued warm interest in the project; their predecessors, Haverford House and Zabel Bros Co., Inc., who for most of the century printed the calendars; Margaret Rauner, for her help in typing the manuscript; and particularly my husband, Roger Scattergood, whose interested listening, clear judgements, and unfailing encouragement, have helped immeasurably to make the compiling of this volume a joyful undertaking.

- *Elizabeth Scattergood*

Selections from a
CENTURY of MOTTOES

Commit thy way unto the Lord; trust also in Him,
    and He shall bring it to pass.

1984   *Psalm 37*

And I said to the man who stood at the gate of
    the year,
"Give me a light, that I may tread safely into the
    unknown."
And he replied, "Go out into the darkness
And put your hand into the hand of God.
That shall be to you better than a light
And safer than a known way."

1942   *Minnie L. Haskins*

Let us be silent that we may hear the whisper of God.

1936   *Ralph Waldo Emerson*

Who knows what opportunity may come to us this
   year? Let us live in a great spirit, then we shall be
   ready for a great occasion.

1982   *The Rev. George Hodges*

If love should count you worthy, and should deign
One day to seek your door and be your guest,
Pause, ere you draw the bolt and bid him rest,
If in your old content you would remain;
For not alone he enters, in his train
Are angels of the mist, the lonely guest,
Dreams of the unfulfilled and unpossessed
And sorrow, and life's immemorial pain!
He wakes in you desires you never may forget.
He shows you stars you never saw before.
He makes you share with him, forevermore,
The burden of the world's divine regret.
How wise were you to open not, and yet
How poor if you should turn him from the door!

1969   *Sidney Lysaght*

And now let us believe in the new year that is given
us — new, untouched, full of things that have
never been.

1980   *Rainer Maria Rilke*

At the edge of history, the future is blowing wildly
in our faces, sometimes brightening the air, and
sometimes blinding us.

1974   *Beth Moore*

History places a burden on our shoulders. It is for
all of us, denying neither the good nor the ills
of the past, to look ahead and not permit old
conflicts to envenom the spirit of the creative
work before us.

1974   *Dag Hammarskjöld*

He who truly goes out to meet the world, goes out
also to God.

1965   *Martin Buber*

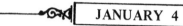

Be at war with your vices
At peace with your neighbor
And let every New Year
Find you a better man.

1948   *Benjamin Franklin*

When in the world are we going to begin to live, as if
    we understood that this is life? This is our time,
    our day -- and it is passing. What are we waiting
    for?

1976   *Richard L. Evans*

God bless thee
Thy goings out, thy comings in
Thy home, thy friends, thy kith and kin
Thy hopes and plans, thy work or rest
God bless thee as He seeth best.
In grief or pain, in joy or cheer
In all He sends, God bless thy year!

1954   *Author Unknown*

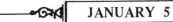

Let gratitude for the past inspire us with trust for the
future.

1957   *François de la Mothe Fénelon*

With God, go over the sea.
Without Him, not over the threshold!

1903   *Russian Proverb*

Greatly begin!   Though thou hast time
For but a line, be that sublime
Not failure, but low aim is crime.

1909   *James Russell Lowell*

Give us courage, and gaiety, and the quiet mind.

1954   *Robert Louis Stevenson*

Let us begin afresh every day.

1956   *St. Catherine of Siena*

Take time to think -- it is the source of power
Take time to play -- it is the secret of perpetual youth
Take time to read -- it is the fountain of wisdom
Take time to pray -- it is the greatest power on earth
Take time to love and be loved -- it is a God-given
   privilege.

1979   *Abridged from "Take Time in the New Year."*

To realize eternity in time means living with intensity
   from moment to moment.

1979   *Damaris Parker-Rhodes*

To Him who sits supreme, let us commit the hour,
   the day, the year -- and fearless view the whole.

1965   *Abigail Adams*

We thank Thee for the increase of the earth
For the rivers and streams
For the sun and moon
For the winds that banish disease
For the herbs and plants that cure the sick
For all things that minister to good and happiness
We pray for a prosperous year to come.
Lastly we give Thee thanks, our Creator and Ruler
In Thee are embodied all things.

1983   *Iroquois Prayer*

It takes three things to attain a sense of significant
   living:
              God
              A soul
              And a moment
              And these things are always here.
              Just to be, is a blessing
              Just to live, is holy.

1981   *Abraham J. Heschel*

Blessed are those who are glad to have time to spare
   for God.

1957   *Thomas à Kempis*

I am glad to think I am not bound to make the world
go right; but only to discover and to do with cheerful heart, the work that God appoints.

I will trust in Him that He can hold His own; and I
will take His will above the work He sendeth me,
to be my chiefest good.

1951   *Jean Ingelow*

It is not the possession of extraordinary gifts that
makes extraordinary usefulness, but the dedication
of what we have to the service of God.

1931   *The Rev. F. W. Robertson*

Take my yoke upon you and learn of Me — for I am
meek and lowly of heart, and ye shall find rest to
your souls.

1886   *Jesus*

I shall pass through this world but once. Any good
thing, therefore, that I can do, or any kindness
that I can show any human being, let me do it
now; but let me not defer or neglect it, for I shall
not pass this way again.

1951   *Stephen Grellet*

Be kind! Remember everyone you meet is fighting
a hard battle.

1957   *Author Unknown*

He that careth for a wounded brother acteth not
alone. There are three in the darkness together,
and the third is the Lord. Blessed is the way of
the helpers, the companions of Christ.

1956   *The Rev. Henry Van Dyke*

Open your eyes, and the whole world is full of God.

1935   *Jacob Boehme*

In the rush and noise of life, as you have intervals,
     step home within yourselves, and be still. Wait
     upon God to feel His presence. This will carry you
     evenly through your day's business.

1951   *William Penn*

Know ye that the Lord, He is God.
It is He who hath made us, and not we ourselves.
We are His people, and the sheep of His pasture.

1973   *Psalm 100*

O God, make us children of quietness, and heirs of
     peace.

1966   *St. Clement*

Search thine own heart
What paineth thee in others
In thyself may be.
All dust is frail, all flesh is weak
Be thou the true man thou dost seek.

1915   *John Greenleaf Whittier*

Here in this actual, wherein thou even now standest
Here or nowhere is thy ideal; work it out therefrom
The ideal is in thyself; the impediment, too, is in
    thyself.

1957   *Thomas Carlyle*

Self conquest is the greatest of victories.

1925   *Plato*

The saints are sinners who keep on trying.

1933   *Robert Louis Stevenson*

Every day is a day of creation. All history is sacred
history. All places are holy places for the true
worshipper.

1975 *Rufus M. Jones*

Our faith is incurably optimistic and unyieldingly
realistic. It teaches us that we live in an ordered
universe in which the moral law of cause and
effect, of means and ends, is as unchangeable as
any physical law. Violence corrupts and destroys
both the user and the victim. The power of love
and non-violence is creative and redeems both.

1967 *American Friends Service Committee*

Cheered by the presence of God, I will do each moment without anxiety, according to the strength
which He shall give me, the work His providence
assigns me.

1956 *Fénelon*

Be still, and know that I am God.

1938   *Psalm 46*

Silently, and almost imperceptibly as the dawn at morning, God makes His presence known.

1966   *Author Unknown*

God remains present to you when you have been sent forth; he who goes on a mission has always God before him; the truer the fulfillment, the stronger and more constant His nearness.

1965   *Martin Buber*

Expect great things from God; attempt great things for God.

1955   *William Carey*

Grant me this day perfectly to begin.

1931   *Thomas à Kempis*

The day is always his who works in it with serenity
    and great aims.

1939   *Ralph W. Emerson*

Well arranged time is the surest mark of a well arranged
    mind.

1953   *Sir Isaac Pitman*

It is they who do their duties in everyday and trivial
    matters who fulfill them on great occasions.

1952   *Charles Kingsley*

The great use of life is to spend it for something that
    outlasts it.

1952   *William James*

Set yourself earnestly to discover what you are made
to do, and then give yourself passionately to the
doing of it.

1983   *The Rev. Martin Luther King, Jr.*

Hold fast to dreams! For if dreams die
Life is a broken-winged bird that cannot fly.
Hold fast to dreams! For when dreams go
Life is a barren field frozen with snow.

1964   *Langston Hughes*

Our age will be remembered, not for its horrifying
crimes, or its astonishing inventions, but because
it is the first generation since the dawn of history
in which mankind dared to believe it practical to
make the benefits of civilization available to the
whole human race.

1964   *Arnold Toynbee*

Is your home a place of rest and refreshment, where
   God himself becomes more real to those who enter
   it?

1955   *Friends' Book of Discipline*

The best way for a man to train up a child in the way
   he should go, is to travel that way himself.

1915   *Author Unknown*

O God,
Give me clean hands, clean words, and clean thoughts
Help me to stand for the hard right against the easy
   wrong
Save me from habits that harm
Teach me to work as hard and play as fairly
In Thy sight alone, as if the whole world saw.
Forgive me when I am unkind.
And help me to forgive those who are unkind to me.
Keep me ready to help others at some cost to myself.
Send me chances to do a little good every day,
And so grow more like Christ.

1955   *A Boy's Prayer (Author Unknown)*

No man has come to true greatness, who has not felt
to some degree that his life belongs to the race.

1937   *The Rev. Phillips Brooks*

If you stoop to be kind, you must swerve often from
your path.

1983   *Mary Webb*

He that turneth from the road to rescue another, turneth toward his goal. He shall arrive by the footpath
of mercy. God will be his guide.

1935   *The Rev. Henry Van Dyke*

To worship rightly is to love each other.

1928   *John G. Whittier*

I am among you as He that serveth.

1948   *Jesus*

Take joy home, and make a place in thy heart for her.

1964   *Socrates*

How easy it is for one benevolent being
To diffuse pleasure around him
And how truly is a kind heart
A fountain of gladness
Making everything in its vicinity
To freshen into smiles.

1949   *Washington Irving*

A joyful heart filled with love is everywhere at home.

1975   *Meister Eckhardt*

Happy is he whose hope is in the Lord.

1934   *Psalm 146*

Great occasions for serving
God come seldom, but little ones
    surround us daily.

1966   *St. Francis de Sales*

I am only one, but I am one
I cannot do everything
But I can do something
What I can do, I ought to do
And what I ought to do
By the grace of God, I will do.

1905   *Canon Farrar*

Whatsoever thy hand findeth to do,
    do it with all thy might.

1933   *Ecclesiastes*

God grant that I may live upon the earth
And face the tasks which every morning brings
And never lose the glory and the worth
Of humble service, and the simple things.

1952   *Edgar A. Guest*

When I consider thy heavens, the
    work of Thy fingers, the moon and
    the stars, which Thou hast ordained;
What is man, that Thou art mindful
    of him? and the son of man, that Thou
    visitest him?
For Thou has made him a little lower than the
    angels, and hast crowned him with glory and honour.

1964   *Psalm 8*

There are many wonders, but nothing more
    wondrous than man.

1964   *Sophocles*

When Christ wished to teach us what God is like,
    he pointed to the God-like in men.

1964   *C. H. C. MacGregor*

Throw not away the hero in thy soul.

1964   *Friedrich Nietzche*

When my courage crumbles
When I feel confused and frail
When my spirit falters
On decaying altars
And my illusions fail

If tomorrow tumbles
And everything I love is gone
I will face regret
All my days, and yet
I will still go on - on.

I go on right then
I go on again
I go on to say
I will celebrate another day
I go on.

1975   *Leonard Bernstein & Stephen Schwartz*

Faith can place a candle in the darkest night.

1936   *Margaret E. Sangster*

Our God whom we serve, is able to deliver us.

1976   *Daniel*

Though wild and loud
And dark the cloud
Behind its folds
His hand upholds
The calm sky of tomorrow.

1897   *The Rev. Martin Luther*

A soul in trouble is near unto God.

1979   *Apocryphal Saying of St. Peter*

For what must be I calmly wait
And trust the path I cannot see
That God is good sufficeth me.

1933   *John G. Whittier*

The greatest calamity may be God's bridgeway to
    the promised land.

1926   *Helen Keller*

Go to sleep in peace; God is awake.

1916   *Victor Hugo*

Beware of despairing about yourself. You are commanded to put your trust in God, not in yourself.

1920   *St. Augustine*

The measure of a man is not determined by his show of outward strength, or the volume of his voice, or the thunder of his action. It is to be seen rather in terms of the strength of his inner self, in terms of the nature and depth of his commitments, the genuineness of his friendships, the sincerity of his purpose, the quiet courage of his convictions, his capacity to suffer, and his willingness to continue "growing up".

1967   *Grady E. Poulard*

The man who stands by his convictions is great in any age.

1965   *John Wanamaker*

Each is the workman of his own future.

1898   *Author Unknown*

Be strong!
We are not here to play, to dream, to drift
We have hard work to do, and loads to lift
Shun not the struggle; face it, 'tis God's gift.

1929   *Maltbie B. Babcock*

The things we have determined wholeheartedly to
   do, are not fulfilled merely by desire, but through
   painful toil.

1945   *Franklin D. Roosevelt*

Be active first thyself
Then seek the aid of heaven
For God helps him who helps himself.

1929   *Euripides*

The reward of one duty is the power to fulfill another.

1927   *George Eliot*

Come ye yourselves apart and rest awhile.

1935   *Jesus*

If you have so much business to attend to that you
   have no time to pray, depend upon it, you have
   more business on hand than God ever intended
   you should have.

1918   *Dwight L. Moody*

Dear Lord and Father of mankind
Forgive our foolish ways
Reclothe us in our rightful mind
In purer lives thy service find
In deeper reverence, praise.

Drop thy still dews of quietness
Till all our strivings cease
Take from our souls the strain and stress
And let our ordered lives confess
The beauty of Thy peace.

1935   *John G. Whittier*

To one fixed point my spirit clings
I know that God is good.

1898   *Author Unknown*

The essential truth concerning God is that He is good.
    To believe that God can order man to commit acts
    of injustice and cruelty, is the greatest mistake it
    is possible to make with regard to Him.

1983   *Simone Weil*

A good end cannot sanctify evil means; nor must
    we ever do evil that good may come of it . . .
    let us then try what love will do.

1983   *William Penn*

Live for God, and do something.

1974   *Mary Lyon*

Good nature and good sense must ever join
To err is human, to forgive divine.

1884   *Alexander Pope*

There is so much bad in the best of us
There is so much good in the most of us
It hardly behooves any of us
To talk about the rest of us!

1906   *John D. Rockefeller's verse*

He who forgives, ends the quarrel.

1929   *African Proverb*

All things whatsoever ye would that men should do
    to you, do ye even so to them.

1885   *Jesus*

JANUARY 30

Three-fourths of the miseries and misunderstandings in the world will disappear if we step into the shoes of our adversaries, and understand their viewpoint.

1929 *Mahatma Gandhi*

Justice between men or between nations can only be achieved through understanding and good will.

1928 *Jane Addams*

Beware of prejudice. Light is good in whatsoever lamp it is burning.

1931 *Abdul Baha*

The day is coming when every man will learn to treat as his own country all the countries of the earth; to recognize in any country he goes to, one of the sacred homes of the human family.

1924 *Paul Richard*

Hast thou named all the birds without a gun?
Loved the wood rose, and left it on its stalk?
At rich men's tables eaten bread and pulse?
Unarmed, faced danger with a heart of trust?
And loved so well a high behavior
In man or maid, that thou from speech refrained
Nobility more nobly to repay?
O, be my friend, and teach me to be thine!

1983   *Ralph Waldo Emerson*

True nobility comes of the gentle heart.

1940   *Dom Michel of Northgate*

Cultivate the universal spirit.

1934   *William Penn*

Who is so low that I am not his brother?
Who is so high that I've no path to him?
Who is so poor that I may not feel his hunger?
Who is so rich that I may not pity him?
Who is so hurt I may not know his heartache?
Who sings for joy my heart may never share?
Who in God's heaven has passed beyond my vision?
Who to hell's depths where I may never fare?
May none, then, call on me for understanding
May none, then, turn to me for help in vain
And drain alone his bitter cup of sorrow,
Or find he knocks upon my heart in vain.

1960   *S. Ralph Harlow*

He that dwelleth in God, dwelleth in love.

1932   *I John, 4*

When we ask God to direct our footsteps, we are to
   move our feet.

1914   *Author Unknown*

The leading rule for a man of every calling is diligence. Never put off till tomorrow what you can
   do today.

1937   *Abraham Lincoln*

The rung of a ladder was never meant to rest upon,
   but only to hold a man's foot long enough to
   enable him to put the other one higher.

1950   *Thomas Huxley*

Lord, Thou knowest how busy I must be today. If
   I forget Thee, do not Thou forget me.

1957   *Sir Jacob Astley*

Where love is
There riches be
Keep us all from poverty.

1955
Medieval Prayer

There is a courtesy of the heart; it is allied to love.
From it springs purest courtesy in the outward
behavior.

1942
Johann Wolfgang von Goethe

True love is but a humble, low-born thing
And hath its food served up in earthenware
It is a thing to walk with hand in hand
Through the everydayness of this workday world
A simple fireside thing, whose quiet smile
Can warm earth's poorest hovel to a home.

1956
James Russell Lowell

Familiar acts are beautiful through love.

1967
Percy Bysshe Shelley

All that I have seen teaches me to trust the Creator
for all I have not seen.

1935   *Ralph Waldo Emerson*

The same old baffling questions!
O, my friend, I cannot answer them.
I have no answer for myself or thee,
Save that I learned beside my mother's knee
"All is of God that is, and is to be,
And God is good." Let this suffice us still
Resting in childlike trust upon His will
Who moves to His great ends, unthwarted by the ill.

1937   *William Cowper*

Consider what St. Augustine said, that he sought God
in himself.   Settle yourself in solitude and you
will come upon Him in yourself.

1935   *St. Theresa*

Ask and ye shall receive
Seek and ye shall find
Knock and it shall be opened unto you.

1885   *Matthew 7*

What I am to be, I am now becoming.

1936   *Author Unknown*

The family is greater than love itself, for it includes, enobles, makes permanent all that is best in love. The pain of life is hallowed by it, the drudgery is sweetened, its pleasures consecrated. It is the trysting place of the generations, where past and future flash into the reality of the present; and it is the great discipline through which each generation learns anew that no man can live for himself alone.

1975   *Pan Pacific Southeast Asia Women's Ass'n.*

Mankind owes to the child the best it has to give.

1976   *U.N. Declaration of the Rights of the Child*

Kindness is the golden chain by which society is bound together.

1931
Goethe

A good deed is never lost. He who sows courtesy reaps friendship; and he who plants kindness gathers love.

1939
Richard Brooke

Kindness lives by something outward expressing something inward; kindness is a sacrament.

1948
The Rev. George Buttrick

Someone hath need of thee.

1949
Author Unknown

What do we live for, if it is not to make life less
    difficult for others?

1914 *George Eliot*

To ease another's heartache is to forget one's own.

1903 *Abraham Lincoln*

Lasting good to our fellow men comes only through
    love and service.

1968 *Harold Evans*

The highest test of the civilization of a race is its
    willingness to extend a helping hand to the less
    fortunate.

1947 *Inscription beneath the bust of*
Booker T. Washington in the Hall of Fame

Nothing but infinite pity is sufficient for the infinite
    pathos of human life.

1964 *H. G. Wood*

I will study and get ready, and maybe my chance will
come.

1917   *Abraham Lincoln*

Nothing worthwhile is lost, by taking time to do it
right

1927   *Abraham Lincoln*

The shortest way to do many things is to do one at
a time.

1950   *The Rev. Richard Cecil*

Are you in earnest? Seize this very minute.
What you can do, or dream you can, begin it.
Boldness has genius, power and magic in it.
Only engage, and then the mind grows heated;
Begin, and then the work will be completed.

1956   *Johann Von Goethe*

Do what you have in hand, and God will show you
what thing is next to do.

1952   *Beneke*

The spirit of man is the candle of the Lord.

1947   *Proverbs 20*

I am not bound to win, but I am bound to be true.
I am not bound to succeed, but I am bound to
live up to what light I have.

1914   *Abraham Lincoln*

The question of success or failure is in the hand of
God.   All that we can do is to release the spirit
of truth.

1947   *Mahatma Gandhi*

The noblest motive is the public good.

1943   *Publius Virgil*

If I have any single belief, it is probably that it is in our nature always to go forward.

1975   *Norman Mailer*

It is difficult to make a man miserable while he feels he is worthy of himself, and claims kindred to the great God who made him.

1982   *Abraham Lincoln*

If we don't change, we don't grow. If we don't grow, we are not really living. Growth demands a temporary surrender of security.

1978   *Gail Sheehy*

In every man there is a king. Speak to the king, and the king will come forth.

1975   *Scandinavian Proverb*

People struggle for a new society when there is vision.

1974   *George Lakey*

I know that the Lord is always on the side of right; but it is my constant anxiety and prayer that I, and this nation, should be on the Lord's side.

1940   *Abraham Lincoln*

If the Lord did not answer prayer, I could not stand it; and if I did not believe in a God who works His will with nations, I should despair of the Republic.

1953   *Abraham Lincoln*

By three things will a nation endure: truth, justice and peace.

1955   *Rabbinical Saying*

True godliness does not turn men out of the world, but enables them to live better in it, and excites their endeavors to mend it.

1958   *William Penn*

With malice toward none, with charity for all; with firmness in the right as God gives us to see the right, let us strive to finish the work we are in: to bind up the nation's wounds, to care for him who shall have borne the battle, and for his widow and his orphan — to do all which may achieve and cherish a just and lasting peace among ourselves and with all nations.

1983   *Abraham Lincoln*

We must come closer together, not only through the modern means of communication; we must come together with our hearts, in mutual understanding, esteem and love. Man must meet man, nation meet nation as brothers and sisters, as children of God.

1966   *Pope Paul VI*

This snow imprisons me; my foolish feet
Refuse to wander on these slippery ways
And I am prone to sigh for summer days.
But when I hear the children on the street
Shouting with laughter in their winter's glee
My soul is glad that not alone for me
Were all things made; else, might the children lose
Half their year's joy, if it were mine to choose.

1912   *Anna Temple*

Love is not simply sentiment or emotion or passion.
    It is readiness to seek the good of another human
    being, and to do it consistently and steadily, and
    if necessary against your own inclinations.

1981   *Anonymous*

The ultimate question for a responsible man to ask
    is . . . how the coming generation is to live.

1979   *The Rev. Dietrich Bonhoeffer*

Love can tell, and love alone
Whence the million stars were strewn
Why each atom knows its own
How in spite of war and death
Gay is life, and sweet is breath.

1957   *Robert Bridges*

The world is full of beauty when the heart is full
of love.

1892   *Author Unknown*

Love sought is good, but given unsought is better.

1948   *William Shakespeare*

I was born to love and not to hate.

1946   *Sophocles*

One loving spirit sets another on fire.

1924   *St. Augustine*

Bear ye one another's burdens, and so fulfill the law
of Christ.

1978   *Galatians 6*

The question of bread for myself is a material question; but the question of bread for my neighbor,
for everybody, is a spiritual and religious question.

1978   *Nicholas Berdyaev*

It seemed to me that if there were hungry children,
something was wrong, and if I did nothing about
it, I would be wrong, too.

1976   *Angela Davis*

May the will of God be done by us
May the love of God be shared by us
May the sons of God be served by us
May this be our honest prayer each day
To work in love, is our way to pray.

1975   *David S. Richie*

All we can do is to make the best of each day.

1948   *Eddie Cantor*

Duty and today are ours.
Results and futurity belong to God.

1941   *Horace Greeley*

Go, do your duty, giving to every task the sublimest
   motive which you can bring to bear upon it. Get
   at the essence of goodness, which is not in its
   enthusiasms or delights, but in its heart of
   consecration.

1941   *The Rev. Phillips Brooks*

The divine moment is the present moment.

1956   *Author Unknown*

Such as are thy habitual thoughts, such also will be
the character of thy mind.

1922   *Marcus Aurelius*

We are what our most cherished thoughts make us.

1925   *Author Unknown*

He who is plenteously provided for from within, needs
but little from without.

1930   *Johann Von Goethe*

Get the pattern of your life from God; then go about
your work and be yourself.

1930   *The Rev. Phillips Brooks*

Self control in trifles trains to self control in crises.

1922   *Author Unknown*

A soft answer turneth away wrath.

1885   *Proverbs*

God bless the good-natured, for they bless everyone else.

1922   *The Rev. H. W. Beecher*

I beseech you that you be worthy of the call, wherewith you are called:

Humble, for the world is God's, not yours;

Meek, for every human being with whom you are brought into contact, is a soul for whom Christ died, a sacred personality;

Patient, for the task is tremendous and men are frail;

Forbearing one another in love, for violence is useless and domination does not help.

1957   *St. Paul (A Modern Translation)*

How little from the resources unrenewable by man, cost the things of greatest value: wild beauty, peace, health and love, and all testaments of spirit!

How simple our basic needs: a little food, sun, air, water, shelter, warmth and sleep!

How lightly might earth bear man forever!

1973   Anonymous

The man who has begun to live more seriously within, begins to live more simply without.

1922   *The Rev. Phillips Brooks*

Live truly, and thy life shall be a great and noble creed.

1938   *Ralph W. Emerson*

Christianity teaches us to care, for God cares.

1938   *Author Unknown*

What doth the Lord require of thee, but to do justly,
   and to love mercy, and to walk humbly with thy
   God?

1942   *Micah 6*

Nor knowest thou what argument
Thy life to thy neighbor's creed has lent
All are needed by each one
Nothing is fair or good alone.

1912   *Ralph W. Emerson*

Kind words are short to speak, but their echoes are
   endless.

1900   *Author Unknown*

Compassion is the chief law of human existence.

1964   *Feodor Dostoevski*

Even before his God may he stand unafraid, whose
heart in truth calls all men brethren.

1931   *Emperor Meyé of Japan*

If we love one another, God dwells in us.

1940   *Zoroaster*

He doeth well, who doeth good
To those of his own brotherhood
He doeth better who doth bless
The stranger in his wretchedness
Yet best, oh best of all, doth he
Who helps a fallen enemy.

1909   *Author Unknown*

Who is my neighbor?   It is he, who near or far, has
need of me.

1929   *Author Unknown*

My first wish is to see the whole world in peace, and
the inhabitants in it as one band of brothers,
striving who should contribute most to the happiness of mankind.

1933   *George Washington*

The spirit of brotherhood, that is still the healer of
the world.

1951   *David Lloyd George*

World peace: loving more, demanding less.

1981   *Ken Keyes, Jr.*

The world is still waiting for a nation "not to be min-
istered unto, but to minister," and thus achieve
immortality.

1981   *The Rev. Andrew Burns Chalmers*

Let us impart all the blessings we ask for ourselves
to the whole family of mankind.

1930   *George Washington*

FEBRUARY 23

O, wad some power the giftie gie us
To see oursel's as ithers see us
It wad frae many a blunder free us
And foolish notion!

1884   *Robert Burns*

Most of the shadows that cross our paths are caused
   by standing in our own light.

1916   *Dinger*

The sages do not consider that making no mistake is
   a blessing. They believe that the great virtue of
   man lies in his ability to correct his mistakes, and
   continually to make a new man of himself.

1976   *Wang Yang-Ming*

Six greatest words on earth:

   Know thyself — Socrates

   Control thyself — Cicero

   Give thyself — Christ

1946   *Author Unknown*

Worry is interest paid on trouble before it is due.

1944   *Dean Inge*

What would you think of the traveller who, instead
   of advancing on his way, was always considering
   the accident he might meet with; and after any
   accident returned to contemplate the scene thereof? Would you not urge him rather to go forward?

1962   *Fénelon*

Hope for the best; be ready for the worst; take with
   calmness what God sends.

1951   *Old Adage*

I believe a sun will pierce the darkest cloud.

                                              Robert Browning

To the quiet mind, all things are possible.

1946   *Meister Eckhart*

The Divine plan for our different lives is like a mosaic, each needed to make the whole.

1943   *Maria C. Scattergood*

A man's religion means the way he is related . . . to God.

1953   *Sir Wilfred Grenfell*

God is the East and the West; and wheresoever ye turn, there is the face of God.
1928   *Mohammed*

Seek, and ye shall find.

1968   *St. Matthew*

To see God in everything makes life the greatest adventure there is.

1953   *Lucille Bordon*

Have thy tools ready
God will find thee work!

1900   *C. Kingsley*

Ways are not scarce, nor chances few
For those who wish God's work to do.

1901   *Author Unknown*

Every duty we omit, obscures some truth we should
   have known.

1893   *John Ruskin*

To find his place and fill it, is success for a man.

1935   *The Rev. Phillips Brooks*

As thy days, so shall thy strength be.

1931   *Deuteronomy 32*

Think not the beautiful doings of thy soul shall perish unremembered. They abide forever, and the good thou doest nobly, truth and love approve. Each pure and gentle deed of mercy brings an honest recompense; and from it looms the sovereign knowledge of thy duty done — a joy beyond all the dignities of earth.

1948   *From the doorway of an old hospital in Philadelphia*

There is no man living who cannot do more than he thinks he can.

1952   *Henry Ford*

Fill us with a gallant and undaunted spirit, that we may be diffusers of life, invigorating all we meet.

1948   *Author Unknown*

When men speak ill of thee
So live that nobody will believe them.

1909   *Plato*

Ne'er suffer sleep thine eyes to close
Before thy mind hath run
O'er every act and thought and word
From dawn to setting sun.
For wrong take shame, but grateful feel
If just thy course hath been.
Such efforts day by day renewed
Will ward thy soul from sin.

1907   *Pupil of Pythagoras*

The only failure a man ought to fear is failure in
    cleaving to the purpose he sees to be best.

1924   *George Eliot*

The man who really does his best is a success whether
    or not the world thinks so.

1926   *Author Unknown*

MARCH 1

In quietness and confidence shall be your strength.

1946   *Isaiah 30*

Let me not pray to be sheltered from dangers
But to be fearless in facing them
Let me not beg for the stilling of my pain
But for the heart to conquer it
Grant that I may not be a coward
Feeling Your mercy in my success alone
But let me feel the grasp of Your hand
In my failure.

1960   *Sir Rabindranath Tagore*

O perfect Love, outpassing sight
O light beyond our ken
Come down through all the world tonight
And heal the hearts of men.

1959   *Laurence Housman*

Every morning lean thine arms upon the window sill
of heaven
Then with the vision in thine heart,
turn to meet the day.

1978   *Author Unknown*

Blessed be Thou, my Lord, for the gift of all Thy
creatures!
And especially for our brother the sun, by whom the
day is enlightened.
He is radiant and bright, and of great splendor,
bearing witness to Thee.

1979   *St. Francis of Assisi*

Surely the spring, when God shall please
Will come again, like a divine surprise.

1977   *Charlotte Mew*

O world invisible, we view thee.
O world unknowable, we know thee.
O world intangible, we touch thee.
The angels keep their ancient places
Turn but a stone, and start a wing
'Tis ye, with your estranged faces
That miss the many-splendored thing.

1957   *Francis Thompson*

He says not "At the end of the way you may find Me."
He says "I am the Way. I am the road under your feet.
The road begins just as low as you happen to be."

1955   *Helen Wodehouse*

"I come in the little things," saith the Lord.
"My starry wings I do forsake
Love's highway of humility to take.
Meekly I fit my stature to your need."

1955   *Evelyn Underhill*

One truth stands firm: All that happens rests on something spiritual. If the spiritual is strong, it creates world history. If it is weak, it suffers world history.

1956   *Dr. Albert Schweitzer*

New times demand new measures and new men; the world advances, and in time, outgrows the laws that in our fathers' day were best; and doubtless after us, some purer scheme will be shaped out by wiser ones than we, made wiser by the steady growth of truth.

1925   *James R. Lowell*

I shall adopt new views as far as they appear to be true views.

1937   *Abraham Lincoln*

Wait not until you are backed by numbers. The fewer the voices on the side of truth, the more distinct and strong must be your own.

1927   *The Rev. William E. Channing*

The great thing in this world is not so much where we
stand as in what direction we are moving.

1925   *Oliver Wendell Holmes*

We live in deeds, not years; in thoughts, not breaths,
In feelings, not in figures on a dial.
We should count time by heart throbs.
He most lives, who thinks most,
Feels the noblest, acts the best.

1957   *P. J. Bailey*

There is no power on earth that can neutralize the
influence of a high, pure, simple and useful life.

1917   *Booker T. Washington*

We are God's fellow-workers.

1978   *1 Corinthians*

Kind hearts are more than coronets.

1928   *Alfred, Lord Tennyson*

Write your name each day in gentleness, kindness,
    patience, courtesy. Good deeds are life's brightest
    stars.

1924   *John Wanamaker*

When generous acts bloom from unselfish thought
The Lord is with us, though we know it not.

1931   *Lucy Larcom*

Help thy brother's boat across, and lo!
thine own has reached the shore.

1946   *Old Hindu Proverb*

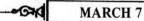

God hath not promised skies always blue
Flower-strewn pathways all our lives through
God hath not promised sun without rain
Joy without sorrow, peace without pain;
But God hath promised strength for the day
Rest for the laborer, light on the way
Grace for the trial, help from above
Unfailing sympathy, undying love.

1944   *Annie J. Flint*

The Lord, He it is that doth go before thee. He will
  be with thee. He will not fail thee, neither forsake thee. Fear not, neither be dismayed.

1950   *Deuteronomy 31*

Dreaming beneath the snow, your heart dreams of
    spring.
Trust the dreams, for in them is hidden the gate to
    eternity.

1957   *Kahlil Gibran*

We may not be chosen to receive God's marching
    orders, or to see the vision from afar, but we may
    well be the seekers. We may break the hold of
    winter on a frozen world, like the wild daffodils
    in the brambles.
Ours may be the joy that sings in the dark places of
    the earth, because even they are filled with the
    glory of God.

1960   *Elfrida Vipont Foulds*

All the flowers of all the tomorrows are in the seeds
    of today.

1960   *Chinese Proverb*

He that is slow to anger is better than the mighty.

1894
                                                    Proverbs 16

Remember that when you are right you can afford to
    keep your temper; and when you are wrong, you
    can't afford to lose it.

1912
                                                Author Unknown

No one should judge another by mere surface facts.
    Until the heart is understood, the actions cannot be.

1921
                                                Author Unknown

The noblest remedy for injuries is forgetfulness.

1890
                                                Author Unknown

Praise loudly; blame softly.

1921
                                                    Catherine II

I met a thousand men on the road to Delhi, and they
were all my brothers.

1933   *Indian Proverb*

There is a principle which is pure, placed in the
human mind, which in different places, hath different names. It is, however, pure, and proceeds
from God. It is deep, and inward, confined to no
form of religion, nor excluded from any where the
heart stands in perfect sincerity. In whomever
this takes root and grows, of what nation soever,
they become brethren.

1982   *John Woolman*

By love, serve one another.

1917   *St. Paul*

What the world needs more than a gigantic leap into
space, is a gigantic leap into peace.

1960

Dwight D. Eisenhower

Every gun that is made, every warship launched,
Every rocket fired signifies in a final sense, a theft
From those who hunger and are not fed,
Those who are cold, and are not clothed.
This is not a way of life;
It is humanity hanging from a cross of iron.

1974

Dwight D. Eisenhower

Let earth rejoice
When all mankind is freed
From man's unreasoning strife
A voice upon the wind cries out
That peace is life.

1952

Author Unknown

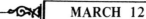

Woodlands that the winters sadden
The leaves of spring again will gladden.
So toils an undiscouraged God
And covers barren hills with sod
And I know nothing that the true,
The good, the gentle cannot do.

1960   *Anonymous*

I find fresh courage for my journeying through every
    troubled year, because of spring.

1959   *Jane Merchant*

Through each wonder of fair days
God himself expresses
Beauty follows all His ways
As the world He blesses
So as He renews the earth
Artist without rival
In His grace of glad new birth
We must seek revival.

1957   *Piae Cantiones (P. Dearmer, Trans.)*

In opening ourselves to God's influence, our greatest
destiny is fulfilled.

1953 *William James*

Is this your fast-to keep the larder lean and clean?
No, 'tis a fast to dole thy sheaf of wheat and méat
Unto the hungry soul.
It is to fast from strife, from old debate and hate
To starve thy sin, not bin;
And that's to keep thy Lent.

1963 *Robert Herrick*

O God, speak to our hearts when men faint for fear,
and the love of many grows cold, and there is
distress of the nations upon earth.
Keep us resolute and steadfast in the things that
cannot be shaken. Restore our faith in the om-
nipotence of good. Renew the love which never
faileth.
And make us to lift up our eyes and behold, beyond
the things which are seen and temporal, the things
which are unseen and eternal.

1968 *The Book of Common Worship (Presbyterian)*

I believe that God can and will bring good out of evil,
  even out of the greatest evil.

1984   *Dietrich Bonhoeffer*

Whoever is born with a loving heart
Dies a-new and a-new.
Wherever hate makes a fatal thrust
Wherever pain spreads its dreary dust
Then must the loving heart atone
Often and often, alone, alone.
To live, it must love
To love, it must give
In giving, dies
Yet in dying, lives.

1979   *Author Unknown*

Jesus understood
The loving reach of God
The longing reach of men
In His life, in His death
He joined their hands together.

1984   *Anonymous*

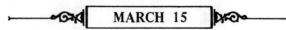

The Lord is gentle and tender, pursuing thee with His love, and following thee up and down with His light.

1967   *Isaac Penington*

He is a path, if any be misled
He is a robe, if any naked be.
If any chance to hunger, He is bread
If any be a bondsman, He is free.
If any be but weak, how strong is He.

1954   *Giles Fletcher*

God is nearer to me than I am to myself.

1964   *Meister Eckhart*

Prayer is the mightiest force in the world.

1948   *Frank Laubach*

A practicing Christian who asks whether he has time
   for prayer is like a carpenter asking whether he
   has time to sharpen his tools.

1957   *Douglas V. Steere*

To pray "Thy will be done" should be no attitude of
   passive submission, but a call to the whole nature
   to strive to the utmost for the cause of God.

1944   *T. Edmund Harvey*

O God, glorify us by letting us do thy work, and
   when it is done, bless us with thy peace.

1961   *Nash*

Man cannot live without some great purpose outside
    himself.

1943   *André Maurois*

The world does not stand still. An eclipse is possible,
    but not an enduring period of night. The church
    began with a few fishermen, a few of the faithful
    in the Catacombs, and the survivors of the arenas
    of Rome.

1957   *Erich Maria Remarque*

He who would valiant be
'Gainst all disaster
Let him in constancy
Follow the Master.
There's no discouragement
Shall make him once relent
His firm avow'd intent
To be a pilgrim.

1957   *John Bunyan*

All the windows of my heart, I open to the day.

1940   *John G. Whittier*

He says to me every morning, "Begin again thy journey and thy life; thy sins, which are many are not
only forgiven, but they shall be made by the
wisdom of God, the basis on which He will build
blessings.

1958   *Thomas Erskine*

You give me today
One minute at a time
That's all I have
All I ever will.

1976   *Christopher Prayers For Today*

Be reverent toward each day.

1964   *Romain Rolland*

Once again the word comes true
Lo, He maketh all things new.

1963   *The Rev. Samuel Longfellow*

He made the heaven and the earth without our aid.
Spring comes again, whether we live or die.
Bringing men to re-birth, He works differently, through
    the souls that are offered to Him to be the chan-
    nels of His will.

1958   *Elizabeth Goudge*

O, Thou who makest the stars
    and turneth the shadow of death
    into the morning, we render Thee the
    tribute of our praise:
        For the resurrection of the springtime
        For the everlasting hopes that rise within
           the human heart
        And for the Gospel which hath brought
           life and immortality to light.

1959   *Dr. William E. Orchard*

Death is not extinguishing the light.
It is putting out the lamp
Because the dawn has come.

1942   *Sir Rabindranath Tagore*

I tell you, there is no death.
We only pass from one season to another.
We must be patient with life for it is eternal.

1963   *Karel Capek*

Never the spirit was born.
The spirit shall cease to be never.
Never was time it was not
End and beginning are dreams.
Birthless, and deathless, and changeless
Remaineth the Spirit forever
Death hath not touched it at all
Dead though the house of it seems.

1918   *Sir Edwin Arnold*

I view death as a great adventure.

1982   *The Rev. Thomas C. Dick*

Courtesy is the sister of charity, the which quencheth
hate, and keepeth love alive.

1984   *St. Francis of Assisi*

This is our poverty —
That we do not belong to each other
Nor serve one another
We go each his own way
And do not care for our neighbor.

We pray thee, O Lord
Redeem us from this estrangement
Redeem us out of this loneliness
Deliver us from the sin that divides us
Join us closely in true love.

1973   *The Church of Germany in Prayer*

May we and all who bear Thy name
By gentle love Thy cross proclaim
Thy gift of peace on earth secure
And for Thy truth the world endure.

1967   *Author Unknown*

Christianity has taught us the true peace and function of suffering. Christ came, and he did not really explain it. He did far more; He met it, willed it, transformed it, and He taught us how to do all this.

1957   *Baron Friedrich von Hügel*

Sorrow cannot be fought and overcome. It cannot be evaded or escaped; it must be lived with.

1955   *Elizabeth Gray Vining*

Where there is sorrow, there is holy ground.
Someday people will realize what that means.
They will know nothing of life til they do.

1977   *Oscar Wilde*

Weeping may endure for a night
But joy cometh in the morning.

1912   *Psalm 30*

The Lord's servant must be gentle towards all.

1898   *St. Paul*

Love alone is capable of uniting living beings in such
    a way as to complete and fulfill them; for it alone
    takes them and joins them by what is deepest in
    themselves.

1984   *Teilhard de Chardin*

Love is a personal sharing in the destiny of another
    person.

1965   *Paul Tournier*

Love has no awareness of merit or demerit.
It does not seek to balance giving and receiving.
Love loves.

1983   *The Rev. Howard Thurman*

The fate of society depends on the education of youth.

1963   *Aristotle*

One good mother is worth a hundred school masters.

1912   *The Rev. George Herbert*

The parent's life is the child's copybook.

1929   *W.E.Partridge*

The most influential of all educational factors is the conversation in a child's home.

1955   *William Temple, Archbishop of Canterbury*

A house is built of bricks and stones
Of sills and posts and piers.
But a home is built of loving deeds
That stand a thousand years.

1914   *Victor Hugo*

Every man's work is always a portrait of himself.

1951   *Samuel Butler*

The load becomes light that is cheerfully borne.

1950   *Ovid*

One of the most durable satisfactions in life is to lose
  oneself in one's work.

1953   *The Rev. Harry Emerson Fosdick*

It is when we forget ourselves that we do things that
  are remembered.

1917   *Author Unknown*

This my task matters for me, and for my fellow men,
  and for eternity.

1983   *Thomas Kelly*

Do right, and leave the results with God.

1951   *Talmadge*

Start where you are with what you have.

1953   *George Washington Carver*

It is not doing things we like to do, but liking the things we have to do, that makes life blessed.

1959   *Johann Von Goethe*

Great works lie not always in our way; but every moment we may do little ones with excellence, that is, with great love.

1958   *St. Francis de Sales*

Reach that which is of God in everyone.

1937   *George Fox*

It is just like an organ, there are white keys and black
    keys; and both are needed to produce great har-
    monies and wonderful music. So it is with the
    races of mankind; all are needed, and God has a
    place for every man no matter what color his skin
    may be.

1946   *James Aggrey*

We must not only affirm the brotherhood of man, we
    must live it.

1937   *Bishop Potter*

He that loveth God, must love his brother also.

1941   *1 John 4*

The way of the spirit, exactly as in the flesh, in a
  world like ours spells labor, hard labor, whatever
  the end we seek.

1946   *Sir Wilfred Grenfell*

Life is not to be equated with survival, but with living
  as God means men to live, serving one another.

1963   *Friends Conference on World Order, 1961*

Thank God our time is now, when wrong comes up to
  face us everywhere, never to leave us till we take
  the longest stride of soul men ever took. Affairs
  are now soul-size. The enterprise is exploration
  into God...

1960   *Christopher Fry*

Wait on the Lord; be of good courage, and He shall
   strengthen thy heart.

1949   *Psalm 27*

I will go anywhere, provided that it is forward.

1914   *David Livingstone*

True greatness is to take the common things of life,
   and walk bravely among them.

1917   *Author Unknown*

It is courage the world needs, not infallibility.

1949   *Sir Wilfred Grenfell*

The residue of life is short; live as on a mountain.

1945   *Marcus Aurelius*

He sang at His bench in Nazareth
While his strong young hands took hold
Of plank and nail to broaden the door
For a shepherd neighbor's fold.
Into His hands on Calvary,
He took the nails again
To make the door which leads to God
Wide for his fellow men.

1961   *Leslie S. Clark*

To be a man is to suffer for others.
God help us to be men!

1977   *Cesar Chavez*

If thou art willing to suffer no adversity, how wilt
    thou be a friend of Christ?

1954   *Thomas á Kempis*

Teach us our kinship with all who have conquered in
    difficulty and loved, even through pain.

1968   *Author Unknown*

Greater love hath no man than this: that a man lay down his life for his friends.

1957   *Jesus*

The victory of death seems very real at times like this; but in the great plan of eternity, death has no victory. These moments pass, and love, which is immortal, remains to solace all mankind.

1941   *Author Unknown*

Peace I leave with you, my peace I give unto you . . . Let not your heart be troubled, neither let it be afraid.

1972   *Jesus*

God is with me night and day
And never turns His face away.

1960   *William Blake*

O, dwellers in the desperate dark
My brothers of the mortal birth
Is there no whisper bids you mark
The Easter of the earth?
Let the great flood of spring's return
Float every fear away, and know
We all are fellows of the fern
And children of the snow.

1978   *Bliss Carman*

Tongues in trees, books in the running brooks
Sermons in stones, and good in everything.

1939   *William Shakespeare*

I saw that there was an ocean of darkness and death,
but an infinite ocean of light and love, which
flowed over the darkness. In that also, I saw the
infinite love of God.

1955   *George Fox*

Give me the pure heart, O Lord
To feel Thy presence near me
Give me the clear mind that understands.

1941   *Author Unknown*

APRIL 2

The future glory of the resurrection begins in this life, as a hidden seed planted in the ground. The new life begins now, right here in the midst of this changing and transient world.

1978   *John LaFarge*

In our era, the road to holiness necessarily passes through the world of action.

1966   *Dag Hammarsjöld*

Do not wait for great strength before setting out. Do not wait to see very clearly before starting. One has to walk toward the light. Take this step! Perform this act!

1963   *Phillippe Vernier*

Think naught a trifle, though it small appear
Sands made the mountain, moments make the year.

1886   *Author Unknown*

Who views eternal meaning in his life
No longer lives unto himself alone
He sees the truth above the dark, grim strife
His risen Lord, whose love will still atone.

1963   *Avery D. Weage*

Therefore, come what may, hold fast to love
Though men should rend your heart
Let them not embitter or harden it
We win by tenderness
We conquer by forgiveness.

1931   *The Rev. F. W. Robertson*

Love is the hardest lesson in Christianity; but for that
   reason it should be most our care to learn it.

1933   *William Penn*

I do not believe that sheer suffering teaches. If suffering alone taught, all the world.would be wise, since everyone suffers. To suffering must be added mourning, understanding, patience, love, openness, and the willingness to remain vulnerable. All these can teach, and can lead to rebirth.

1974   *Anne Morrow Lindbergh*

There is no "getting over" sorrow, but there is "getting into" sorrow, and finding right in the heart of it, the dearest of all human beings — the Man of Sorrows.

1974   *Forbes Robinson*

Beneficient streams of tears flow at the finger of pain
And out of the clouds that smile, beneficient rivers of rain.

1976   *Robert L. Stevenson*

The darkness now seems absolute; men before us have forgotten that it hides the morning star.

1945   *Irwin Edman*

The dawn is not distant, nor is the night starless.
Love is eternal!
God is still God, and his Faith shall not fail us.
Christ is eternal!

1917   *Henry W. Longfellow*

Life eternal is to know that God is Love, and that nothing can separate those who love. In recognizing this truth, death loses its reality.

1945   *Emily V. Hammond*

Calvary is a telescope through which we look into the long vistas of eternity, and see the love of God breaking forth into time.

1982   *The Rev. Martin Luther King, Jr.*

They say everyone has his own cross to bear, Lord, and You once said "Take up your cross and follow Me." What do these things mean? I think they mean that every person ultimately has to face up to reality -- face his own destiny, his own calling, his own nature and responsibilities. The way of the Cross was Your understanding of Your mission, and Your faithfulness to it.

1967   *Michael Boyd*

Freedom is seen to be not a matter of what we want to do, but rather finding out what it is that has the strongest claim on our desire and our loyalty, and then making our choices serve that end. Finally we discover that freedom is a kind of obedience.

1964   *Stephen Bayne*

The best gift that a man can make to mankind is his best self.

1924   *Author Unknown*

Sing, men and angels, sing
For God, our Life and King
Has given us light and spring
And morning breaking.
Now may man's soul arise
As kinsman to the skies
And God unseals his eyes
To an awakening.

After the winter snows
A wind of healing blows
And thorns put forth a rose
And lilies cheer us
Life's everlasting spring
Has robbed death of its sting
Henceforth a cry can bring
Our Master near us.

1980   *John Masefield*

In Him was life, and the Life was the Light of men.

1957   *St. John*

The day which you fear as being the end of all things,
    is the birthday of your eternity.

1970   *Seneca*

Awake, thou wintry earth, fling off thy sadness
Ye vernal flowers, laugh forth your ancient gladness
A new and lovely tale throughout the land is sped
It floats o'er hill and dale to tell that death is dead.

1954   *Thomas Blackburn*

Despite the suffering, despair and ugliness created by
racial conflicts, national rivalries, food shortages
and pollution, the bells of Easter always lift me
on waves of hope. To experience a spring day is
enough to assure me that eventually life will
triumph over death.

1974   *René Dubois*

Good enduringly practiced must overcome evil.

1974   *Stephen G. Cary*

He was born in an obscure village, the child of a peasant woman. He grew up in another village, where He worked in a carpenter shop until He was thirty. Then for three years He was an itinerent preacher. He never wrote a book. He never held an office. He never had a family or owned a home. He didn't go to college. He never visited a big city. He never traveled two hundred miles from the place where He was born. He did none of the things that usually accompany greatness. He had no credentials but Himself. He was only thirty-three when the tide of public opinion turned against Him. His friends ran away. One of them denied Him. He was turned over to His enemies and went through the mockery of a trial. He was nailed to a cross between two thieves. While He was dying. . . His executioners gambled for His garments, the only property He had on earth. When He was dead, He was laid in a borrowed grave through the pity of a friend.

Nineteen centuries have come and gone, and today He is the central figure of the human race. All the armies that ever marched, all the navies that ever sailed, all the parliaments that ever sat, all the kings that ever reigned, put together, have not affected the life of man on this earth as much as that. . . ONE SOLITARY LIFE

1982   *The Rev. James A. Francis*

After Jesus lived and died in it, the world was never
the same again. A new and spiritual energy enter-
ed the process of human life. It is not exhausted --
it will never be exhausted.

1960
Middleton Murry

He brought light out of darkness
He can bring summer out of winter
All occasions invite His mercies
And all times are His seasons.

1979
The Rev. John Donne

The greatest thing that Jesus Christ demonstrated
was giving love in return for hatred.

1982
Paramahansa Yogananda

We know that we have passed out of death into
life because we love the brethren.

1977
1 John 3

Who hath not learned in hours of faith
The truth, to flesh and sense unknown
That life is ever lord of death
And love can never lose its own.

1961   *John G. Whittier*

When the evening of this life comes, we shall be
  judged on love.

1955   *St. John of the Cross*

Time and death shall depart
And say in flying
Love has found a way to live
By dying!

1977   *John Dryden*

Whether you understand it or not, God loves you.

1982   *Thomas Merton*

O flower, whose fragrance tender with sweetness
    fills the air
Dispel in glorious splendor, the darkness everywhere;
True man, yet very God, from sin and death now
    save us
And share our every load.

1963   *Speier Gebetbuch, 1599*

The conquest of death is the final achievement of
   religion; no religion is worth its name unless it
   can prove itself more than a match for death.

1961   *L. P. Jacks*

Now is the time of gladness
To sing of the Lord's goodness.

1963   *Trans. from Latin by Miles Coverdale*

They helped every one his neighbor, and everyone
said to his brother "Be of good courage."

1943   *Isaiah 41*

Look around you
Find someone in need
Help somebody to-day.

1963   *Author Unknown*

The smallest good deed is better than the grandest
intention.

1942   *Anonymous*

I find life an exciting business, and most exciting
when it is lived for others.

1944   *Helen Keller*

When we give what we have, the Lord makes it
enough.

1961   *Lady Frances Balfour*

Many men owe the grandeur of their lives to their tremendous difficulties.

1934   *Charles H. Spurgeon*

One man finds an obstacle a stumbling block; another finds it a stepping stone.

1938   *William Lyon Phelps*

Be sure to put your feet in the right place and then stand firm.

1929   *Abraham Lincoln*

It is the nature of man to rise to greatness, if greatness is expected of him.

1959   *John Steinbeck*

In simple trust like theirs who heard
Beside the Syrian sea
The gracious calling of the Lord
Let us like them, without a word
Rise up and follow Thee.

1945   *John G. Whittier*

He who would imitate the Master in bringing in the
    Kingdom of Heaven, will find his life filled with
    humble and simple duties.

1963   *Silvanus P. Thompson*

No man or woman, even of the humblest sort, can
    really be strong, gentle, pure, and good, without
    the world being better for it; without somebody
    being helped and comforted by the very existence
    of that goodness.

1978   *The Rev. Phillips Brooks*

Every task, however simple
Sets the soul that does it free
Every deed of love and mercy
Done to man is done to Me.

1931 *The Rev. Henry Van Dyke*

Be sure that if you do the very best in that which is
  laid upon you daily, you will not be left without
  sufficient help when some weightier occasion
  arises.

1932 *Jean Nicolas Grou*

Do not despise your situation. In it you must act,
  suffer and conquer. From every point of earth,
  we are equally near to heaven and the Infinite.

1947 *Henri-Frédéric Amiel*

Lo, the fair beauty of earth from death of the winter
   arising!
Every good gift of the year, now with its Master
   returns.

1975   *Venantius Honorius Fortunatus*

Sunrise to sunset changes now
For God doth make His world anew.

1975   *St Clement of Alexandria*

It is eternity now. I am in the midst of it. It is
   about me in the sunshine.

1974   *Richard Jefferies*

Fair are the meadows
Fairer still the woodlands
Robed in the blooming garb of spring.
Jesus is fairer, Jesus is purer
Who makes the wo'ful heart to sing.

1980   *Crusaders' Hymn*

Does the world owe you a living?   Or do you owe
   it a life?

1914   *Author Unknown*

Conscience is nothing else than the echo of God's
   voice within the soul.

1925   *Author Unknown*

Go put your creed into your deed.

1927   *Ralph W. Emerson*

The submergence of self in the pursuit of an idea,
   the readiness to spend oneself without measure
   prodigally, almost ecstatically, for something
   great and noble, to spend oneself one knows
   not why -- some of us like to believe that this
   is what religion means.

1933   *Justice Benjamin Cardozo*

Man's primary allegiance is to his vision of truth,
and he is under obligation to affirm it.

1943   *Jane Addams*

God offers to every mind its choice between truth
and repose. Take which you please - you can
never have both.

1974   *Ralph W. Emerson*

It fortifies my soul to know
That though I perish, truth is so;
That howso'er I stray and range
Whate'er I do, Thou dost not change.
I steadier step when I recall
That if I slip, Thou dost not fall.

1962   *Arthur Clough*

Truth crushed to earth shall rise again;
The eternal years of God are hers.

1962   *William Cullen Bryant*

Faith is the great motive power, and no man realizes his full possibilities unless he has the deep conviction that life is eternally important, and that his work well done is part of an unending plan.

1931   *Calvin Coolidge*

I affirm my faith in the kingdom of God, and my hope in its final triumph. I determine to carry its spirit and laws into all my dealings in the world that now is.

1941   *A Creed from the Federal Council of*
Churches of Christ in America

God will always show His will to one who is willing to do it.

1935   *Unknown*

Love is the moving power of life.

1982   *Paul Tillich*

Wisdom is oft-times nearer when we stoop, than
    when we soar.

1944   *William Wordsworth*

No noble impulse is wasted.

1901   *Author Unknown*

A pity beyond all telling
Is hid in the heart of love.

1967   *William Butler Yeats*

All we have to do to preserve the heroic in men, is to set them fighting their real enemies; and the real enemies of mankind are ignorance, disease, superstition and war.

1936   *Frederick K. Stamm*

Christianity has not failed. It is simply that nations have failed to try it. There would be no war in a God-directed world.

1938   *Admiral Byrd*

Not until we can love all men, all races, all so-called nationalities as Christ loved them, are we on the road to peace on earth.

1942   *Sir Wilfred Grenfell*

How beautiful upon the mountains are the feet of him that bringeth good tidings, that publisheth peace.

1973   *Isaiah 52*

A judicious silence is always better than truth spoken without charity.

1908   *Author Unknown*

When angry count ten before you speak; when very angry count one hundred.

1909   *Author Unknown*

Our anger and impatience often prove much more mischievous than the things about which we are angry or impatient.

1912   *Marcus Aurelius*

A wise man revenges himself for injuries by kindness.

1933   *Chinese Proverb*

Judge not thy friend until thou standest in his place.

1930   *Rabbi Hillel*

If you want to put the world right, start with yourself.

1931   *Author Unknown*

The greatest help to overcoming mistakes is to acknowledge them.

1938   *Author Unknown*

Almost everyone you meet knows more on some subject than you do. Turn that side of him toward you, and absorb all you can.

1912   *Author Unknown*

Man becomes civilized when he listens. He listens when he is ready to be moved by ideas.

1961   *William Ernest Hocking*

My own principle has always been, where two paths are open to take the more venturesome.

1956   *Sir Wilfred Grenfell*

Man is by no means a completely finished product. Man is only what God is planning, a projected design.

1964   *Nicholas Berdyaev*

Every child comes with a message that God is not discouraged of man.

1961   *Rabindranath Tagore*

Where would our tomorrows be without the children of today?

1964   *Unicef Calendar, 1963*

The youth of a nation are the trustees of posterity.

1950   *Benjamin Disraeli*

God oft hath a large share in a small house.

1941   *The Rev. George Herbert*

I found Him very easily among the pots and pans.

1955   *St. Theresa*

Bless the four corners of this house
And be the lintel blest
And bless the hearth, and bless the bread
And bless each place of rest.
And bless the door which opens wide
To strangers as to kin
And bless each crystal window pane
That lets the sunlight in
And bless the rooftree overhead
And every sturdy wall
The Peace of Man, the Peace of God,
The Peace of love on all.

1955   *Arthur Guiterman*

What you are is God's gift to you. What you make of
   yourself is your gift to Him.

1942   *Author Unknown*

Be not simply good.
Be good for something.

1948   *Henry D. Thoreau*

The diamond cannot be polished without friction,
   nor man perfected without trials.

1950   *Chinese Proverb*

What thou art in the sight of God, that thou truly
   art.

1951   *Thomas à Kempis*

Kind words produce their own image in men's souls, and a beautiful image it is. They sooth and quiet and comfort the hearer. We have not yet begun to use kind words in such abundance as they ought to be used.

1953   *Blaise Pascal*

The kindly word that falls to-day, may bear its fruit tomorrow.

1951   *Mahatma Gandhi*

Hail! Ye small sweet courtesies of life! For smooth do ye make the road of it.

1961   *Laurence Sterne*

Let the law of kindness know no limits.

1961   *General Advices - Society of Friends*

If you would know God, be not therefore a solver of riddles; rather, look about you, and you shall see Him playing with your children.

1957   *Kahlil Gibran*

I sought to hear the voice of God
And climbed the topmost steeple
But God declared "Go down again!
I dwell among the people."

1960   *Newmark*

I have come to know God by serving Him.

1956   *Tukaram*

Be to men's virtues very kind
Be to their faults a little blind.

1884   *Matthew Prior*

Friendship lightens the burden of adversity by
   dividing and sharing it.

1941   *Cicero*

We often do more good by our sympathy than
   by our labours.

1916   *Canon Farrar*

The glory of friendship is not the outstretched
   hand, nor the kindly smile, nor the joy of
   companionship; it is the spiritual inspiration
   that comes to one when he discovers that
   someone else believes in him, and is willing
   to trust him.

1982   *Ralph W. Emerson*

Bloom, frozen Christian, bloom!
May stands before thy door!

1957   *Angelus Silesius*

For lo! the winter is past
The rain is over and gone
The flowers appear on the earth
The time of the singing of birds is come
And the voice of the turtle is heard in the land.

1983   *Song of Soloman*

There is no unbelief
Whoever plants a seed beneath the sod
And waits to see it push away the clod
He trusts in God.

1933   *Lizzie York Case*

The glory of the Lord is always new -- every hour,
     every morning, every spring!

1964   *John Hoyland*

Not in the clamor of the crowded street
Not in the shouts and plaudits of the throng
But in ourselves, are triumphs and defeat.

1938   *Henry W. Longfellow*

There is only one man that can be responsible for my
    conduct, and that is myself.

1940   *Henry J. Cadbury*

Have a purpose in life, and having it, throw into your
    work such strength of mind and muscle as God has
    given you.

1936   *Thomas Carlyle*

Determine that the thing can and shall be done, and
    then we shall find a way.

1936   *Abraham Lincoln*

The only genuine elite in this world, or in the next,
    is the elite of those men and women who have
    given their lives to justice and charity.

1965   *Sargent Shriver*

Do what your conscience tells you to be right, and
leave the consequences to God.

1927   B. R. Haydon

Keep your courage up, and conversely, it will keep
you up!

1932   L. L. Eames

He who would gather roses must not fear thorns.

1948   Dutch Proverb

Let no man falter who thinks he is right.

1974   Abraham Lincoln

Thou Comrade of my soul
So near, yet ever just beyond my sight
Reach back Thy hand to hold me in the night
And bring me to the goal.

1946   E. F. Howard

In the economy of God, no effort, however small, put
  forth in the right cause fails of its effect.

1916   *John G. Whittier*

Success consists in doing the common things of life
  uncommonly well.

1949   *Author Unknown*

Life is not made up of great sacrifices and duties; but
  of little things in which smiles and kindness and
  small obligations given habitually are what win and
  preserve the heart.

1952   *Sir Humphrey Davy*

All service ranks the same with God.
There is no last nor first.

1931   *Robert Browning*

The work of the world does not wait to be done by
    perfect people.

1983   *Author Unknown*

Do the duty that lies nearest thee; the next is already
    clearer..

1909   *Thomas Carlyle*

God obligeth no man to do more than he hath given
    him ability to perform.

1983   *The Koran*

Duty done is the soul's fireside.

1935   *Browning*

He said not that we should not be tempted, nor tra-
vailed, nor afflicted, but he promised "Thou shalt
not be overcome."

1956   *Lady Julian of Norwich*

I know not what the future hath
Of marvel or surprise
Assured alone that life and death
His mercy underlies.

I know not where His islands lift
Their fronded palms in air
I only know I cannot drift
Beyond His love and care.

1890   *John G. Whittier*

Thou wilt keep him in perfect peace whose mind is
stayed on Thee because he trusteth in Thee.

1953   *Isaiah 26*

The earth is the Lord's, and the fulness thereof.

1977   *Psalm 24*

As the marsh hen secretly builds on the watery sod
Behold, I will build me a nest on the greatness of
    God.
I will fly in the greatness of God as the marsh hen
    flies
In the freedom that fills all the space
'Twixt the marsh and the skies
By so many roots as the marsh grass sends in the
    sod
I will heartily lay me a-hold on the greatness of
    God.

1955   *Sidney Lanier*

I came from God, I belong to God, I return to God.

1967   *Ignatius Loyola*

MAY 8

Show mercy whenever it is in your power. Mercy is
    one of the attributes of God.

1983   *William Penn*

Yours are the eyes through which to look out Christ's
    compassion to the world.
Yours the feet with which He is to go about doing
    good
And yours the hands with which He is to bless us
    now.

1954   *St. Teresa*

Our neighbor is every man without exception.

1964   *Very Rev. Mother Marie des Douleurs*

Blessed are the merciful.

1941   *Jesus*

Good temper, like a sunny day, sheds brightness
over everything.

1890   *Author Unknown*

All the rust of life ought be scoured off by mirth.

1920   *Oliver W. Holmes*

There are souls in the world which have the gift of
finding joy everywhere, and of leaving it behind
them wherever they go.

1941   *The Rev. Frederick Faber*

What big things hang on a smile and a cheery word,
no man can ever say.

1979   *Sir Wilfred Grenfell*

Blessed are the happiness makers!

1937   *The Rev. Henry Ward Beecher*

Love is to the mortal nature what the sun is to the earth.

1975

Honoré de Balzac

Every beautiful thing has been loved into being.

1942

The Rev. Joseph F. Newton

You cannot love without giving.

1912

Author Unknown

No love is wasted.

1940

Carolena Wood

Give me strength to make my love fruitful in service.

1946

Rabindranath Tagore

No man is an island, entire of itself
Every man is a piece of the continent, a part of the
    main
Any man's death diminishes me,
Because I am involved in mankind.

1960   *The Rev. John Donne*

I am not an Athenian or Greek, but a citizen of the
    world.

1980   *Socrates*

God grant that not only the love of liberty, but a
    thorough knowledge of the rights of man may
    pervade all nations of the earth, so that a phil-
    osopher may set his foot anywhere on its surface
    and say "This is my country."

1952   *Benjamin Franklin*

Democracy is based upon the conviction that there
are extraordinary possibilities in ordinary people.

1959   *The Rev. Harry E. Fosdick*

The ideals of democracy have never been dream pic-
tures, but goals.   The way forward toward our
goals we will find only through our own exertions;
through tireless, patient and courageous exertion.

1944   *Sigrid Undset*

The peace testimony teaches us to absorb violence
without returning it, and by presenting an oppo-
nent with a peaceful example, to lead him out of
his violence.

1972   *Curtis Bok*

There is one thing that is stronger than armies, and
that is an idea whose time has come.

1917   *Victor Hugo*

Listen to the long stillness
New life is stirring
New dreams are on the wing
New hopes are being readied
Mankind is fashioning a new heart
Mankind is forging a new mind
God is at work
This is the season of promise.

1976   *The Rev. Howard Thurman*

Truth doth flourish as the rose, and the lilies do grow
among the thorns, and the plants atop of the
hills; and upon them the lambs do skip and play;
and never heed the tempests, nor the storms,
floods nor rains, for...Christ is over all, and doth
reign. And so be of good faith, and valiant for
the truth.

1983   *George Fox*

Awake, awake to love and work
The lark is in the sky!

1962   *G. A. Studdert-Kennedy*

With every rising of the sun
Think of your life as just begun.

1937   *Author Unknown*

Begin the day by offering it and yourself to God.
Look to the day as an individual thing which
begins and ends with completeness in itself;
then take this thing, this day, and offer it to
God to be a day for His use.

1976   *George S. Stewart*

If men will do their utmost,
God will not fail to do His share.

1946   *Jacob A. Riis*

We plant a tree this day
And leave the blossoming to God.

1950   *Aimée Thomas*

The worship of God is not a rule of safety; it is an
   adventure of the spirit.

1958   *Alfred North Whitehead*

Not one holy day, but seven
Worshipping, not at the call of a bell
But at the call of my soul
Singing, not at the baton's sway
But to the rhythm of my heart
Loving, because I must
Giving, because I cannot keep
Doing, for the love of it.

1950   *Lorenzo Henry*

I do not ask for either crosses or consolations
I simply present myself before Thee
I open my heart to Thee.

1977   *François Fénelon*

God does not work in all hearts alike, but according to the preparation and sensitivity He finds in each.

1962   *Meister Eckhart*

Slowly, through all the universe, that temple of God is being built wherever, in any world, a soul by free-willed obedience catches the fire of God's likeness. When, in your hard fight, in your tiresome drudgery, or in your terrible temptation, you catch the purpose of your being and give yourself to God, and so give Him the chance to give Himself to you, your life, a living stone, is taken up and set into the growing wall.

1962   *The Rev. Phillips Brooks*

That we are alive to-day is proof positive that God has something for us to do to-day.

1982   *Anna R. Lindsay*

Civilization has to be rebuilt in every age, just as each
of us has to make a new beginning every morning
of each day.

1967   *John Nef*

What makes a city great and strong?
Not architecture's graceful strength
Not factories' extended length
But men who see the civic wrong
And give their lives to make it right
And turn its darkness into light.

1910   *Author Unknown*

Real life must have some heroic force in it, else
it only breathes but does not live.

1966   *Horace Bushnell*

He believed that one man can make a difference,
and that every man should try.

1967   *Jacqueline Kennedy of John F. Kennedy*

Learn to see what you look at.

1937   *Kilgus*

Each day as I look, I wonder where my eyes were
    yesterday.

1974   *Bernard Berenson*

The more I study nature, the more I stand amazed
    at the work of the Creator. I pray while I am
    engaged in my work in the laboratory.

1928   *Louis Pasteur*

Every beautiful finite thing is a window by which the
    soul may catch a kindling, inspiring glimpse of
    the Eternal.

1941   *Rufus M. Jones*

If thou of fortune be bereft
And in thy store there be but left
Two loaves; sell one, and with the dole
Buy hyacinths to feed thy soul.

1984   *James T. White*

Everyone is the son of his own works.

1915   *Miguel de Cervantes*

Search me, O God, and know my heart; try me and
    know my thoughts; and see if there be any wicked
    way in me, and lead me in the way everlasting.

1966   *Psalm 139*

You cannot run away from a weakness. You must
    sometime fight it out or perish. And if that be
    so, why not now, and where you stand?

1918   *Robert L. Stevenson*

God writes His poems in transformed lives.

1925   *Author Unknown*

True spirituality consists in believing in the power of good, rather than that of ill.

1969   *Nicholas Berdyaev*

No longer talk at all about the kind of man that a good man ought to be, but be that man.

1966   *Marcus Aurelius*

Keep, therefore, within the centre, and stir not from the presence of God revealed within thy soul.

1938   *Jacob Boehme*

Life develops from within.

1936   *Elizabeth Browning*

Be swift to love; be slow to hate.

1932   *Author Unknown*

Hatred never yet was overcome by hatred
But hatred is always overcome by love.

1928   *Buddha*

One who is free from hatred requires no sword.

1951   *Mahatma Gandhi*

To turn all that we possess into the channels of
    universal love becomes the business of our lives.

1935   *John Woolman*

Cast all your care on God. That anchor holds.

1938   *Alfred, Lord Tennyson*

Whate'er may vex or grieve thee
To Him commit thy ways
Who friendless will not leave thee
Whom highest heaven obeys.
By Him the clouds are guided
The winds arise and blow
By Him the path provided
Whereon thy feet may go.

1955   *St. Matthew Passion - J. S. Bach*

By the grace of God, anyone can carry his burden
    until nightfall; anyone can do his work for one
    day.

1916   *Author Unknown*

I will never leave thee, nor forsake thee.

1938   *Hebrews 13*

All that pleases is for a moment
All which troubles is for a moment
That only is important which is eternal.

1960   *Inscription on a doorway of Milan Cathedral*

Thou, O God, hast made us for Thyself; and our
    hearts are restless until they find rest in Thee.

1946   *St. Augustine*

Speak to Him, thou, for He hears
And spirit with spirit can meet.
Closer is He than breathing
And nearer than hands and feet.

1929   *Alfred, Lord Tennyson*

Prayer is not to ask what we wish of God, but what
    God wishes of us.

1945   *A 16th Century Mystic*

Friendship is a sheltering tree.

1939   *Samuel Taylor Coleridge*

Just to realize that there are friends in the world who
    care is a great help.

1936   *Sir Wilfred Grenfell*

We are all travellers in the wilderness of this world,
    and the best that we can find in our travels is an
    honest friend.

1947   *Robert L. Stevenson*

Go oft to the house of thy friend, for weeds choke
    up the unused path.

1950   *Author Unknown*

The light of friendship is like the light of phosphorus,
    seen when all around is dark.

1946   *Crowell*

The vital point about religion, after all, is not what
you think about it, but what you do about it.

1941 *Sir Wilfred Grenfell*

The world is not yet made; do your share to-day.

1920 *Author Unknown*

May we ourselves be those who help to make the
world progress.

1931 *Zoroaster*

So near is grandeur to dust
So near is God to man
When duty whispers low "Thou must"
The youth replies "I can".

1915 *Ralph W. Emerson*

Lord, set my life in order, making me to know
what I ought to do, and do it in the way that
I should.

1941 *St. Thomas Aquinas*

God's ways seem dark, but soon or late
They touch the shining hills of day
The evil cannot brook delay
The good can well afford to wait.

1980   *John G. Whittier*

I do not fear to tread the path I cannot see
Because the hand of One who loves is leading me.

1967   *Nyata*

When you are at you wits' end, you'll find God lives
   there.

1978   *Old Saying*

They that wait upon the Lord shall renew their
   strength.   They shall mount up with wings as
   eagles;   they shall run and not be weary, and
   they shall walk and not faint.

1968   *Isaiah*

It is a glorious destiny to be a member of the human race, though it is a race dedicated to many absurdities, and one which makes many mistakes; yet, with all that, God Himself gloried in becoming a member of the human race.

1981   *Thomas Merton*

We live in this world when we love it.

1973   *Rabindranath Tagore*

Let your senses explore the wonder of creation
Let your mind feel the presence of today
Let your soul beat in rhythm to the song of celebration
And let love be the music that you play.

1976   *A folk song called Joy*

I have learned
To look on nature, not as in the hour
Of thoughtless youth, but hearing oftentimes
The still, sad music of humanity,
Not harsh nor grating, though of ample power
To chasten and subdue. And I have felt
A presence that disturbs me with the joy
Of elevated thoughts; a sense sublime
Of something far more deeply interfused
Whose dwelling is the light of setting suns,
And the round ocean and the living air
And the blue sky, and in the mind of man
A motion and a spirit that impels
All thinking things, all objects of all thought,
And rolls through all things.

1977   *William Wordsworth*

Everything that lives is holy. Life delights in life.

1978   *William Blake*

There lives no man on earth who may always have
rest and peace with no troubles and crosses, with
whom things go always according to his will.
There is always something to be suffered here,
consider it as you will.

1967   *Theologia Germanica*

No one has reached maturity until he has learned to
face the fact of his own death, and shaped his
way of living accordingly.

1967   *Bradford Smith*

He will shield you from suffering, or send you unfailing strength with which to bear it.

1978   *St. Francis de Sales*

Though my soul may set in darkness
It will rise in perfect light
I have loved the stars too fondly
To be fearful of the night.

1976   *Sarah Williams*

O Lord, we ask Thee not to be safe, but to be faithful.

1962 *Prayer of martyred Kikuyu Christians*

Life is girt all around with contributions of men who
   have perished to add their point of light to our
   sky.

1963 *R. W. Emerson*

Being blind and deaf to the material world has helped
   me develop an awareness of the invisible, spiritual
   world. I know my friends, not by their physical
   appearance, but by their spirit. Consequently,
   death does not separate me from my loved ones.
   To me there is no such thing as death, in the
   sense that life has ceased.

1962 *Helen Keller*

Death is no more than a turning of us over from
   time to eternity.

1967 *William Penn*

What is God?
In the universe, law;
In the conscience, goodness;
In the mind, truth;
In nature and art, beauty and order;
In the heart, love.

1967   *Bradford Smith*

You are to me, O Lord, what wings are to the flying
bird.

1966   *A disciple of Ramakrishna*

Blessed art thou, O Lord our God, King of the universe, who givest strength to the weary.

1966   *The Hebrew Prayer Book*

The grateful soul of the wise man is the true altar
of God.

1974   *Philo Judaeus*

God is the wind and we are the sails. It is necessary
to give ourselves to the wind, to accept, and to
be not afraid.

1960   *Peter Greave*

At every season, voyager, yet find
Paths to the farthest reaches of the mind;
The stars still constant through the transient gloom
The heart still eager, and the course still true
In worlds expanding, and the Word's duration.

1964   *John Bechervaise*

Nature is the living, visible garment of God.

1975   *Johann Wolfgang von Goethe*

All things created on earth sing to the glory of God.

1978   *Venantius Fortunatus*

In times of change, we must avoid both ignorant change, and ignorant opposition to change.

1951   *John Stuart Mill*

Force never changed anybody's mind; but education and understanding have won a lot of victories, even though they take longer.

1951   *Charles E. Wilson*

An open mind leaves a chance for someone to drop a worthwhile thought in it.

1953   *Quoted in "Hand In Hand"*

The world is slowly learning that because two men think differently, neither need be wicked.

1944   *Sir Wilfred Grenfell*

All nations smile in the same language.

                                         Author Unknown

Is it too much to dream that one day a nation's prestige might be based on greatness through service, rather than on greatness through power?

1961   *Colin W. Bell*

Mankind's sole salvation lies in making everything his business.

1974   *Alexander Solzhenitsyn*

We shall do our part to build a world of peace, where the weak are safe, and the strong are just. We are not helpless before that task, or hopeless of its success.

1964   *John F. Kennedy*

The greatest power in the world is the power of an idea.

1949   *Gen. Douglas Mac Arthur*

Be patient enough to live one day at a time, as Jesus
taught us, letting yesterday go, and leaving tomorrow until it arrives.

1949   *The Rev. Joseph Fort Newton*

Don't let yesterday use too much of to-day.

1952   *Author Unknown*

My part is to improve the present moment.

1953   *The Rev. John Wesley*

It takes only half as much time to do a thing when it
should be done, as will be required a week later.

1953   *E. W. Howe*

Deliver me from all fretfulness.
Give me a stout heart to bear my own burdens.
Give me a willing heart to bear the burdens of others.
Give me a believing heart to cast all burdens upon
Thee.

1970   *Dr. John Baillie*

The only thing necessary for the triumph of evil, is for good men to do nothing.

1969   *Edmund Burke*

If you would like to build a better world, start in your own community.

1948   *Crime Prevention Magazine*

The world belongs to the energetic.

1925   *Ralph W. Emerson*

The more one has to do, the more one is able to accomplish.

1950   *Sir Thomas Buxton*

If at first you do succeed, try something harder!

1959   *Ernest Ligon*

Only a life lived for others is a life worthwhile.

1950   *Dr. Albert Einstein*

It is one of the most beautiful compensations of
    life, that no man can sincerely try to help another
    without helping himself.

1952   *J. Pearson Webster*

The equality of man can only be accomplished by
    the sovereignty of God. The longing for frater-
    nity can never be satisfied, but under the sway of
    of a common Father.

1943   *Benjamin Disraeli*

Therefore, all things, whatsoever ye would that men
    should do to you, do ye even so to them.

1917   *Jesus*

Behavior is a mirror, in which everyone shows his image.

1934   *Johann Wolfgang von Goethe*

Handsome is, that handsome does.

1930   *Oliver Goldsmith*

The way to fare well, is to do well.

1887   *Author Unknown*

It matters not what you are thought to be, but what you are.

1909   *Author Unknown*

There is only one way by which we can reach our desired goal - that is, to get up and go!

1915   *Author Unknown*

No longer forward nor behind
I look in hope or fear
But grateful, take the good I find
The best of now and here.

1885   *John G. Whittier*

Riches are not from the abundance of worldly goods,
   but from a contented mind.

1964   *Sayings of Mohammed*

Who is wise? He that learns from everyone.
Who is powerful? He that governs his passions.
Who is rich? He that is content.

1934   *Benjamin Franklin*

The happiness of your life depends upon the character of your thoughts.

1989   *Author Unknown*

I found Him in the shining of the stars
I marked Him in the flowering of His fields.

1954   *Alfred, Lord Tennyson*

Over the shoulders and slopes of the dunes
I saw the white daisies go down to the sea
A host in the sunshine, an army in June
The people God sends to set our hearts free.
The bobolinks rallied them up from the dell
The orioles whistled them out of the wood.
And all of their singing was "Earth, it is well,"
And all of their dancing was "Life thou art good."

1957   *Bliss Carman*

Happiness was made to be shared.

1932   *Jean Racine*

Blessed are the pure in heart for they shall see God.

1914   *Jesus*

Though we travel the world over to find the beauti-
    ful, we must carry it with us, or we find it not.

1939   *Ralph W. Emerson*

I pray the prayer of Plato old
God make thee beautiful within.

1927   *John G. Whittier*

May the long time sun shine upon you,
All love surround you
And the pure light within you
Guide you on your way.

1974   *A Yoga Chant*

Suffer the little children to come unto Me, and forbid them not, for of such is the Kingdom of Heaven.

1980   *Jesus*

To have parents who love each other is the best gift that children can have.

1979   *Damaris Parker-Rhodes*

The most personal immediate action faithful members of Christ's body can take, is to love little children and to help others...love them.

1973   *The Rev. Joseph A. Howell*

O, God, who hast set the solitary in families, who dost join man to man in friendship, grant us Thy gift of understanding.

1980   *The Rev. Elmore M. McKee*

Where mercy, love, and pity dwell
There God is dwelling too.

1954   *William Blake*

He drew a circle that shut me out
Heretic, rebel, a thing to flount
But love and I had the wit to win
We drew a circle that took him in.

1923   *Edwin Markham*

To love is nothing else than to wish that person good.

1956   *St. Thomas Aquinas*

All within the four seas are brethren.

1928   *Confucius*

A golden dream was sent to dreamers two
One scorned the dream, the other made it true.

1921   *Author Unknown*

Every great and commanding moment in the annals
   of the world, is the triumph of some enthusiasm.

1932   *Ralph W. Emerson*

Patience and diligence, like faith, remove mountains.

1926   *William Penn*

The work an unknown good man has done, is like a
   vein of water flowing hidden underground, secretly making the ground green.

1920   *Thomas Carlyle*

That cause can neither be lost nor stayed
Which takes the course of what God has made,
And is not the trusting in walls and towers
But slowly growing from seed to flowers.
Be then no more by a storm dismayed
For by it the full grown seeds are laid
And though the tree by its might it shatters
What then, if thousands of seeds it scatters?

1965   *Kristian Ostergaard*

If I am sure of anything, it is that the world's troubles
    will retreat before the steady effort of persons
    who seek the truth.

1966   *Edmund B. Spaeth, Jr.*

This is the vision of a great and noble life;
To endure ambiguity in the moment of truth
And to make light shine through it.
To stand fast in uncertainty
To prove capable of unlimited love and hope.

1974   *Karl Jaspers*

There are two ways of living; a man may be casual and simply exist, or constructively and deliberately try to do something with his life. The constructive idea implies constructiveness not only about his own life, but about that of society, and the future possibilities of mankind.

1974   *Julian Huxley*

If things are ever to move upward, someone must be ready to take the first step, and assume the risk of it.

1960   *William James*

There is a spirit, and a need, and a man, at the beginning of every great human advance.

1984   *Coretta Scott King*

Stir up the gift of God which is in thee.

1947   *II Timothy*

Religion is the inborn longing of the human soul for God, and for companionship with Him. It is as fundamental as life itself, as enduring as the human race.

1958   *John D. Rockefeller, Jr.*

Whoever comes to Me, through whatsoever form, I reach him. All men are struggling through paths which in the end lead to Me.

1974   *The Bhagavad-Gita*

You need not seek Him here or there. He is no farther off than the door of the heart.

1974   *Meister Eckhart*

Who trusts in God's unchanging love
Builds on the rock that naught can move.

1959   *Georg Neumark*

Great Spirit, help me never to judge another, until I
  have walked two weeks in his moccasins.

1960   *A Sioux Indian's Prayer*

I'll not willingly offend
Nor be easily offended.
What's amiss I'll try to mend
And endure what can't be mended.

1898   *Author Unknown*

Repay an evil action with a generous one.

1941   *The Rev. Joseph Fort Newton*

Nothing is so strong as gentleness,
Nothing so gentle as real strength.

1906   *St. Francis de Sales*

Take life as you find it, but don't leave it so.

1932   *Author Unknown*

We are judged not by the degree of our light, but by
   our fidelity to the light we have.

1939   *William E. Channing*

I will not cut my conscience to fit the fashions of our
   times.

1981   *Lillian Hellman*

Sometimes we must give up the obvious good for the
   somehow strangely better.

1978   *Bliss Forbush*

Our greatest glory consists not in never falling, but in
   rising every time we fall.

1965   *Oliver Goldsmith*

To live is to go on.

1967   *Rufus M. Jones*

Whoso draws nigh to God through doubtings dim
God will advance a mile in blazing light to him.

1962   *Author Unknown*

Never more thou needest seek Me
I am with thee everywhere
Raise the stone, and thou shalt find Me
Cleave the wood, and I am there.

1939   *The Rev. Henry van Dyke*

We are called beyond strain, to peace and power and
   joy and love through abandonment of self. We are
   called to put our hand trustingly in His hand, and
   walk the holy way, in no anxiety, assuredly resting
   in Him.

1966   *Thomas Kelly*

God hath made of one blood all nations of men for
   to dwell on the face of the earth.

1923   *St. Paul*

We are each responsible to all, for all.

1974   *Feodor Dostoevski*

All men are brothers, all receive blessings of the same
   heaven.   The suffering of others is my suffering.
   The good of others is my good.

1974   *A Shinto Text*

Thou our Father, Christ our brother,
All who live in love are Thine.
Teach us how to love each other
Lift us to the joy divine.

1940   *The Rev. Henry van Dyke*

Great ideas come into the world as gently as doves. If we live attentively, we shall hear amid the uproar of empires and nations a faint flutter of wings, the great stirring of life and hope.

1963   *Albert Camus*

What matters is that one be for a time inwardly attentive.

1963   *Anne Morrow Lindbergh*

A monent's insight is sometimes worth a life's experience.

1984   *Oliver W. Holmes*

The more faithfully you listen to the voice within you, the better you will hear what is sounding outside.

1984   *Dag Hammarsjöld*

There is no duty we so underrate as the duty of being
happy. By being happy we sow benefits upon the
world which remain unknown to ourselves.

1922   *R. L. Stevenson*

The real sources of joy in this life are not the results
of easy tasks, but of hard ones.

1946   *Sir Wilfred Grenfell*

Go not abroad for happiness, for see
It is a flower blooming at thy door!
Bring love and justice home, and then no more
Thou'lt wonder in what dwelling joy may be.
Dream not of noble service elsewhere wrought
The simple duty that awaits thy hand
Is God's voice uttering a divine command
Life's common deeds built all that saints have
wrought.

1959   *The Rev. Minot Savage*

Truth is the beginning of all good.

1901

Author Unknown

What is true, simple and sincere, is most congenial to men's nature.

1975

Cicero

Beware of half truths; you may get hold of the wrong half.

1962

S. Selvaratnam

Never depart in your conduct from your honest convictions.

1901

Author Unknown

The truth is always the strongest argument.

1952

Sophocles

Speak your truth quietly and clearly...and listen to others.

1983

Desiderata

First of all, have patience.

1974   *Rainer Maria Rilke*

Neither despise nor oppose what thou dost not understand.

1962   *William Penn*

Never lose a holy curiosity.

1975   *Dr. Albert Einstein*

Whosoever would understand what he hears must hasten to put into practice what he has heard.

1963   *St. Gregory*

The kingdom of heaven is at hand, not be ushered in by some radical social revolution, but just by you and me discovering who we really are, and acting accordingly.

1974   *The Rev. Arthur Foote*

Our doubts are traitors, and make us lose the good we
  oft might win, by fearing to attempt.

1929
                                        William Shakespeare

Yesterday is dead - forget it.
Tomorrow does not exist - don't worry.
Today is here - use it.

1918
                                        Author Unknown

Take what is
Trust what may be
That's life's true lesson.

1939
                                        Robert Browning

Help us always to trust in Thy goodness; that walking
  with Thee and following Thee in all simplicity, we
  may possess quiet and contented minds, and may
  cast all our care on Thee, for Thou carest for us.

1961
                                        Christina Rossetti

To the wrong that needs resistance
To the right that needs assistance
To the future in the distance
Give yourself.

1903   *Author Unknown*

No task is too little to be done in the best way.

1902   *Author Unknown*

I long to accomplish a great and noble task, but it
   is my chief duty to accomplish humble tasks as
   though they were great and noble.   The world
   is moved along, not only by the mighty shoves
   of its heros, but also by the aggregate of the tiny
   pushes of each honest worker.

1958   *Helen Keller*

Grant that each of us may pass something on to the
   unknown future to make the world a little better.

1979   *F. W. Norwood*

Live from day to day, even from hour to hour.
Perseverance is one of the crowning graces of God.

1965

Baron Friedrich von Hügel

It is not the leap at the start, but the steady going on
    that gets there.

1965

John Wanamaker

Look ahead.
You are not required to complete the task,
Neither are you permitted to lay it down.

1966

The Talmud

Not for one single day
Can I discern the way.
But this I know:
Who gives the day
Will show the way
So I securely go.

1930

John Oxenham

God has created me to do Him some definite service
He has committed some work to me which He has
    not committed to another.
I have my mission; I have a part in a great work.
I am a link in the chain, a bond of connection be-
    tween persons.
He has not created me for naught.
I shall do good,
I shall do His work.

1975   *Cardinal Newman*

Nothing is more powerful than an individual acting
    out of his conscience, thus helping to bring the
    collective conscience to life.

1983   *Norman Cousins*

I would fain be to the Eternal Goodness, what his
    own hand is to a man.

1953   *Theologia Germanica*

The time for seeking God is always now.

1957

Douglas V. Steere

I sought Thee at a distance, and did not know that Thou wast near. I sought Thee abroad in Thy works, and behold, Thou wast in me.

1955

St. Augustine

It is in devotion to this search after the Most High - a search which may assume an infinity of varied forms - that the dedicated life consists; the life not to be judged by apparent failure to reach some fixed and rigid goal, but rather by the quality of its striving.

1968

Lord Haldane

And ye shall seek Me and find Me, when ye shall search for Me with all your heart.

1983

Jeremiah

Christ's spirit taketh breath again
Within the lives of holy men.

1960   *W. C. Braithwaite*

There are some men and women in whose company
we are always at our best. Here are sanctifiers of
souls; here, breathing through the common clay,
is heaven.

1958   *The Rev. Henry Drummond*

Who moves the world, first moves a single soul.

1962   *Charles F. Robinson*

Blessed are they which do hunger and thirst after
righteousness, for they shall be filled.

1966   *Jesus*

1884.

BE to Men's Virtues very kind,
to their Faults a little Blind. *Prior.*

O wad some power the giftie gie us
To see oursel's as ithers see us:
It wad frae mony a blunder free us,
And foolish notion! *Burns.*

Keep thy heart with all diligence,
for out of it are the issues of LIFE.

MAY···1884.

Sun.	Mon.	Tue.	Wed.	Thur.	Fri.	Sat.
✢	✢	✢	✢	1	2	3
4	5	6	7	8	9	10
11	12	13	14	15	16	17
18	19	20	21	22	23	24
25	26	27	28	29	30	31
✢	✢	✢	✢	✢	✢	✢

Thomas Scattergood — Compiler 1884 - 1908

ALL THE RUST OF LIFE OUGHT TO BE SCOURED OFF BY MIRTH.
O. W. HOLMES.

THE GREATER THE DIFFICULTY THE MORE GLORY IN SURMOUNTING IT;
SKILFUL PILOTS GAIN THEIR REPUTATION FROM STORMS AND TEMPESTS.
EPICURUS.

IF OUR LOVE WERE BUT MORE SIMPLE
WE SHOULD TAKE HIM AT HIS WORD;
AND OUR LIVES WOULD BE ALL SUNSHINE
IN THE SWEETNESS OF OUR LORD.
FABER.

WE CAN NOT MAKE THE SUNSHINE, BUT WE CAN
REMOVE FROM THAT WHICH CASTS A SHADOW ON US.
SPURGEON.

ILL DEEDS ARE DOUBLED WITH AN EVIL WORD.
SHAKESPEARE.

1920	OCTOBER				10th Mo.	
SUN	MON	TUE	WED	THU	FRI	SAT
TRIFLES MAKE PERFECTION—					1	2
3	4	5	6	7	8	9
10	11	12	13	14	15	16
17	18	19	20	21	22	23
24	25	26	27	28	29	30
31	BUT PERFECTION IS NO TRIFLE.					

J. Henry Scattergood — Compiler 1909 - 1952

LOVE MEANS TAKING UP OTHER LIVES INTO OUR OWN.
—ANONYMOUS

REJOICE NOT WHEN YOUR ENEMY FALLS,
NEVER EXULT WHEN HE IS OVERTHROWN;
IF YOUR ENEMY IS HUNGRY GIVE HIM FOOD,
AND GIVE HIM WATER IF HE THIRSTS;
FOR SO YOU SHALL QUENCH BLAZING PASSIONS,
AND THE ETERNAL WILL REWARD YOU. —PROVERBS

LOVE FEELS NO BURDEN, THINKS NOTHING OF TROUBLE,
ATTEMPTS WHAT IS ABOVE ITS STRENGTH, PLEADS NO EXCUSE
OF IMPOSSIBILITY.
THOUGH WEARY, LOVE IS NOT TIRED;
THOUGH PRESSED, IT IS NOT STRAITENED;
THOUGH ALARMED, IT IS NOT CONFOUNDED.
—THOMAS À KEMPIS

1958		JUNE				6th Mo.
SUN	MON	TUE	WED	THU	FRI	SAT
1	2	3	4	5	6	7
8	9	10	11	12	13	14
15	16	17	18	19	20	21
22	23	24	25	26	27	28
29	30					

LOVE DIVINE, ALL LOVES EXCELLING, JOY OF
HEAVEN TO EARTH COME DOWN; FIX IN US THY HUMBLE DWELLING.
—CHARLES WESLEY

Elizabeth and A. Burns Chalmers — Compilers 1953 - 1981

THE MORE FAITHFULLY YOU LISTEN TO THE VOICE WITHIN YOU, THE
BETTER YOU WILL HEAR WHAT IS SOUNDING OUTSIDE.

DAG HAMMARSJÖLD

I BELIEVE THAT AN INDIVIDUAL'S GREATEST PRIDE, AS WELL AS HIS
GREATEST CONTRIBUTION TO SOCIETY, MAY LIE IN THE WAYS IN
WHICH HE IS DIFFERENT FROM ME, AND FROM OTHERS, RATHER
THAN IN THE WAYS HE CONFORMS TO THE CROWD. I SHALL
THEREFORE ACCEPT THOSE DIFFERENCES AND ENDEAVOR TO BUILD A
USEFUL RELATIONSHIP UPON THEM.   LINTON B. SWIFT

WHOE'ER FEELS DEEPLY, FEELS FOR ALL WHO LIVE.

MADAME DE STAEL

SENSE YOUR POWER TO LIFT THE MOOD OF DESPAIR.

KEN KEYES, JR.

1984	AUGUST	8th Mo.

SUN	MON	TUE	WED	THU	FRI	SAT
THE POOR DESERVE			1	2	3	4
5	6	7	8	9	10	11
12	13	14	15	16	17	18
19	20	21	22	23	24	25
26	27	28	29	30	31	

NOT JUST SERVICE AND DEDICATION, BUT ALSO THE JOY
THAT BELONGS TO HUMAN LOVE.   MOTHER TERESA

Elizabeth Scattergood — Compiler 1982 - present

I count this thing to be grandly true
That a noble deed is a step toward God

1926   *J. G. Holland*

The secret of success is constancy of purpose.

1952   *Benjamin Disraeli*

I will live with all my might while I live.

1955   *Dwight L. Moody*

Cultivate the tree which you have found to bear fruit
   in your soil.

1960   *Henry D. Thoreau*

A tiny seed can fill a field with flowers.

1971   *Author Unknown*

The only limit to our realization of tomorrow will be
  our doubts of to-day. Let us move forward with
  strong and active faith.

1946   *Franklin D. Roosevelt*

Don't be afraid of opposition. Remember, a kite
  rises against, not with, the wind.

1943   *Hamilton Mabie*

The dogmas of the quiet past are inadequate to the
  stormy present. The occasion is piled high with
  difficulty, and we must rise with the occasion.

1962   *Abraham Lincoln*

The true patriot is never content with things as they
  are.

1963   *Naomi Gillman*

Nations have no existence apart from their people. If every person in the world loved peace, every nation would love peace. If all men refused to fight one another, nations could not fight one another.

1935   *J. Sherman Wallace*

The dream of the philosopher to-day is often the creed of the persecuted minority to-morrow; the day following to become the faith of a nation.

1919   *Author Unknown*

What are you doing to understand and remove the causes of war, and develop conditions and institutions of peace?

Do you live in that life and power which takes away the occasion of all wars?

Do you seek to take part in the ministry of reconciliation between individuals, groups and nations?

1956   *Friends Book of Discipline*

My fellow Americans, ask not what your country will
   do for you; ask what you can do for your country.

1961   *John F. Kennedy*

The strength of a democracy is judged by the quality
   of the service rendered by its citizens.

1955   *Plato*

O beautiful, our country, 'round thee in love we draw
Thine is the grace of freedom, the majesty of law
Be righteousness thy scepter, justice thy diadem
And in thy shining forehead, be peace the crowning
   gem.

1961   *The Rev. Frederick L. Hosmer*

JULY 5

The peace of this world is always uncertain unless men keep the peace of God.

1965   *T. S. Eliot*

If our world is to survive in any sense that makes survival worth while, it must learn to love, not to hate; to create, not to destroy.

1952   *King George VI*

The past cannot be changed; the future is still in your power.

1950   *Hugh White*

When one knows Thee
Then alien there is none
Then no door is shut.

1961   *Rabindranath Tagore*

Every war, even for the nation that conquers, is nothing less than a misfortune.

1916 *Gen. von Moltke*

If you had seen but one day of war, you would pray God you might never see another.

1916 *Duke of Wellington*

Give the children a true idea of war in their history books, and the next generation would no more want a war than they would want an earthquake.

1922 *Israel Zangwill*

The more I study the world, the more I am convinced of the inability of force to create anything durable. Alexander, Caesar, Charlemagne, and I, myself, have founded empires; but upon what did these creations depend? They depended upon force. Jesus Christ founded His empire upon love, and to this very day millions would die for Him.

1917 *Napoleon*

To those who fear that an enemy will destroy us and
    what we love,
To those who build shelters that will not shield
Who trust armed might that has no power
And defense that cannot defend:
We say there is a power, within man and beyond man
That can yet save us, and with which we cannot be
    moved.

This power is released by the vision of our heart in
    repentance
And by the fusion of our minds and a common search
    for truth and justice
It can break out into the world even from a single
    person
Who can start a chain reaction in those around him.

Let us therefore turn finally and personally
From our preoccupation with developing a capacity
    to kill
To discovering anew the capacity to change
And to building world institutions which transcend
    nationalism
And help us to identify with all humanity as brothers
Seeking to bring the fruit of peace to all men.

1978   *Kenneth Boulding*

The tide of public opinion is already beginning to
rise. As it one day swept away slavery, so it will
one day rise and sweep even the old god Mars off
his pedestal.

1918   *Lester Jayne*

These things shall be, a loftier race
Than e'er the world hath known, shall rise
With flame of freedom in their souls,
And light of knowledge in their eyes.
They shall be gentle, brave and strong
To spill no drop of blood, but dare
All that may plant man's lordship firm
On earth and fire and sea and air
Nation with nation, land with land,
Unarmed shall live as comrades free.
In every heart and brain shall throb
The pulse of one fraternity.

1959   *J. Addington Symonds*

Blessed are the peacemakers, for they shall be called
the children of God.

1884   *Jesus*

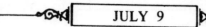

It matters not if this ideal city of which we speak has ever been, or in fact will ever be; he who has seen it will live in the manner of that city.

1973

Socrates

While there is a remnant, however small, who care intensely for the quality of the community's life, there is hope.

1973

The Rev. Henry Sloane Coffin

I ask for daily bread, but not for wealth
    Lest I forget the poor.
I ask for strength, but not for power
    Lest I despise the meek.
I ask for wisdom, but not for learning
    Lest I scorn the simple.
I ask for a clean name, but not for fame,
    Lest I contemn the lowly.
I ask for peace of mind, but not for idle hours
Lest I fail to hearken to the call of duty.

1973

Inazo Nitobe

He will not fail, nor be discouraged until He have set
  justice in the earth.

1964   *Isaiah*

The pearl of justice is found in the heart of mercy.

1964   *St. Catherine of Siena*

We seek a reign of love, in which the wounds of past
  injustices will not be used as excuses for new ones;
  where racial barriers will be eliminated, so that the
  stranger will be sought and welcomed, where every
  man will be received as a brother.

1964   *1963 Chicago Conference on Religion and Race*

If a man be gracious and courteous to strangers, it
  shows he is a citizen of the world.

1952   *Francis Bacon*

Do you know that you are God's temple, and that
God's spirit makes its home in you?

1956

I Corinthians

What is conscience? It is the guardian of the very
best within us.

1940

Rom Landau

Do not get out of bed until you have set your
thoughts on God. Remind yourself that He is waiting
to illumine your spirit each morning as you awake.

Never get into bed with a burdened or heavy mind.
Night is a holy time, a time for renewing and refreshment.

1963

Muriel Lester

And God, who studies each separate soul
Out of commonplace lives makes His beautiful whole.

1945

Susan Coolidge

The world, after all our science...is still a miracle.

1964   *Thomas Carlyle*

Field and forest, vale and mountain
Blossoming meadow, flashing sea
Chanting bird, and flowing fountain
Call us to rejoice in Thee.

1959   *The Rev. Henry van Dyke*

I have a need in me for all things holy
The stir of God in ocean and in wood
Where evil slips away, and surely, slowly
The closed heart opens to the homing good.

1945   *Eleanor Baldwin*

I have not known a day without a cloud
Nor have I known a night without a star
For always love is near, and prayer is heard
And faith and love abide.

1965

J. Ritchie Smith

Deep peace of the running wave to you
Deep peace of the flowing air to you
Deep peace of the quiet earth to you
Deep peace of the shining stars to you
Deep peace of the Son of Peace to you.

1954

Fiona MacLeod

Make it mine
To feel amid the city's jar
That there abides a peace of Thine
Man did not make and cannot mar.

1910

Matthew Arnold

Like the sun, love shines everywhere.

1974   *The Rev. Arthur Foote*

Love suffereth long, and is kind
Love vaunteth not itself, is not puffed up;
Doth not behave itself unseemly, seeketh not her
    own
Is not easily provoked; thinketh no evil
Rejoiceth not in iniquity, but rejoiceth in the truth;
Beareth all things, believeth all things,
Hopeth all things, endureth all things
Love never faileth.

1968   *I Corinthians*

Order your lives in love.

1966   *Motto of the International*
                                  Eucharistic Congress, 1964

Every life is meant to help all lives.

1897   *Alice Cary*

Kindness is catching, and if you go around with a
    thoroughly developed case, your neighbor will
    be sure to get it.

1922   *Author Unknown*

If someone is too tired to give you a smile, just give
    him one of yours anyway; for nobody needs a
    smile as much as one who has none left to give.

1939   *Author Unknown*

Do unto others, as though you were the others.

1933   *Elbert Hubbard*

Whosoever would become great among you shall be
    your minister; and whosoever would be first among
    you shall be your servant.

1965   *St. Matthew*

I heard the voice of the Lord saying, "Whom shall I
 send, and who will go for Us?" Then said I, "Here
 I am, send me."

1953   *Isaiah 6*

When we are really honest with ourselves, we must
 admit that our lives are really all that belong to us;
 so it is how we use our lives that determines
 what kind of men we are. It is my deepest belief
 that only by giving our lives, do we find life. I am
 convinced that the truest act of courage, the
 strongest act of manliness, is to sacrifice ourselves
 for others in a totally non-violent struggle for justice.

1977   *Cesar Chavez*

By love serve one another.

1917   *St. Paul*

Life touched by God cares not what serves or helps
 itself, but what will help mankind.

1911   *Thomas à Kempis*

There are no gains without pains.

1901   *Benjamin Franklin*

From my limited point of view I can't hope to under-
    stand the enormous mysteries of life. I can try to
    approach them with love and compassion. I can
    try to lessen, at least a little, the pain and suffering
    about me.

1976   *Christopher Prayers for Today*

In championing a cause, there is profound power in
    the willingness to accept suffering in oneself,
    rather than inflict it on others.

1975   *Stephen Cary*

The opportunity now exists to change the course of
    human events. We hope you will join us.

1978   *Clamshell Alliance Opposed to Nuclear War*

Diligence is the mother of good fortune.

1931   *Miguel de Cervantes*

The man who does his job well tones up the whole
    society; and the man who does a slovenly job,
    whether he is a janitor or a judge, a surgeon or a
    technician, lowers the tone of the society.

1961   *John Gardner*

The best things are nearest: breath in your nostrils,
    light in your eyes, duties at your hand, the path
    of God before you. Then do not grasp at the
    stars, but do life's common work, certain that dai-
    ly duties and daily bread are the sweetest things in
    life.

1964   *Robert L. Stevenson*

If thou hast yesterday thy duty done
And thereby cleared firm footing for today
Whatever clouds make dark tomorrow's sun
Thou shalt not miss the way.

1894   *Author Unknown*

Dost thou love life? Then do not squander time, for that is the stuff that life is made of.

1894   *Benjamin Franklin*

He has the deed half done, who has made a beginning.

1979   *Horace (65 B.C.)*

A man is a little thing, while he works by and for himself; but when he gives voice to the rules of love and justice, he is Godlike.

1946   *Ralph W. Emerson*

Ten men banded together in love can do what ten thousand separately would fail in.

1935   *Thomas Carlyle*

Our todays make our tomorrows.

1957   *The Rev. Minot Savage*

Kindly deeds and thoughts and words
Bless the world like songs of birds.

1901 *Author Unknown*

Mercy is twice blessed; it blesses him that gives and
  him that takes.

1897 *William Shakespeare*

A poor man served by thee
Shall make thee rich.
A sick man helped by thee
Shall make thee strong.
Thou shalt be served thyself,
By every sense of service which thou renderest.

1913 *Elizabeth B. Browning*

Light up a fire of love in thy soul.

1964 *Jalalu'ddin Rumi*

To thine own self be true
And it must follow as the night the day
Thou canst not then be false to any man.

1914

William Shakespeare

Do not think of your faults, still less of others! Look
   for what is good and strong, and try to imitate it.
   Your faults will drop off like dead leaves, when
   their times come.

1943

John Ruskin

Associate reverently, and as much as you can with
   your loftiest thoughts.

1935

Henry D. Thoreau

Teach me, O God, not to torture myself...through
   stifling reflection, but rather teach me to breathe
   deeply in faith.

1963

Søren Kierkegaard

There is that near you which will guide you.
O wait for it, and be sure to keep to it.

1968   *Isaac Penington*

God reveals himself to us when we listen to his guid-
    ance; God reveals himself through us when we
    share our guidance with others.

1950   *Emily V. Hammond*

Prayer is loving attention to God.

1963   *The Cloud of Unknowing*

Trust in the Lord with all thine heart, and lean not
    unto thine own understanding. In all thy ways
    acknowledge Him, and He shall direct thy paths.

1983   *Proverbs*

Come what may
Time and the hour run
through the roughest day.

1940   *William Shakespeare*

Trouble does not last always.

1940   *Old Negro Spiritual*

Let us be of good cheer, remembering that the misfor-
    tunes hardest to bear, are those which never come.

1935   *James R. Lowell*

Set thy heart aright and constantly endure
And make not haste in time of trouble
For gold is tried in the fire,
And acceptable men in the furnace of adversity.
Believe in Him, and He will
help thee order thy way aright,
And trust in Him.

1963   *Ecclesiasticus*

Let him that seeketh cease not until he finds.

1938   *From an old Papyrus*

While not optimistic, I am hopeful. By this I mean
    that hope, as opposed to cynicism and despair, is
    the sole precondition for a new and better life;
    and hope arouses, as nothing else can arouse,
    a passion for the possible.

1979   *The Rev. William S. Coffin*

Someday, after mastering the winds, the waves, the
    tides, and gravity, we shall harness for God the
    energies of love; and then for the second time in
    the history of the world, man will have discovered
    fire.

1979   *Teilhard de Chardin*

Great deeds cannot die
They, with the sun and moon
Renew their light.

1940   *Alfred, Lord Tennyson*

I am certain of nothing but the holiness of the heart's
affection and the truth of imagination.

1974   *John Keats*

Thanks to the human heart by which we live
Thanks to its tenderness, its joy and fears
To me the meanest flower that blows can give
Thoughts that do often lie too deep for tears.

1974   *William Wordsworth*

O Thou, from whose unfathomed law
The year in beauty flows
Thyself the vision passing by
In crystal and in rose
Day into day doth utter speech
And night to night proclaim
In ever-changing worlds of light
The wonder of Thy name.

1964   *Frances W. Wile*

God is our refuge and strength.

1938   *I Timothy 6*

I bind unto myself to-day
The power of God to hold and lead
His eye to watch, His might to stay
His ear to hearken to my need!
The wisdom of my God to teach
His hand to guide, his shield to ward
The word of God to give me speech
His heavenly host to be my guard.

1959   *St. Patrick's Breastplate*

Alone with none but Thee, my God
I journey on my way
What need I fear when Thou art near
O King of night and day?
More safe am I within Thy hand
Than if a host did round me stand.

1965   *Attributed to St. Columba*

God hath made of one blood all nations for to dwell
on the face of the earth.

1941   *Acts 17*

Now is the time to dare to practice mercy
Enough wounds have been struck in strife
But He who serves us and reconciles us with God
Wishes that we become brothers on God's earth.

1956   *Hymn used in a conference in West Germany,*
1951

Create in us the splendor that dawns
    when hearts are kind
That knows not race nor color as
    boundaries of the mind!
That learns to value beauty in heart
    or brain or soul
And longs to bind God's children
    into one perfect whole.

1961   *S. Ralph Harlow*

Liberty implies duty, not privilege.

1967   *Albert Camus*

Through concern for the freedom of others, our own
    heritage is best preserved and strengthened.

1963   *J. Irwin Miller*

Long as thine art shall love true art
Long as thy science truth shall know
Long as thine eagle harms no dove
Long as thy law by law shall grow
Long as thy God is God above
Thy brother every man below
So long, dear land of all my love,
Thy name shall shine, thy fame shall glow.

1967   *Sidney Lanier*

A sense of national purpose is at bottom a sense of
    international purpose.

1961   *Clinton Rossiter*

The workshop of character is everyday life.

1975   *Maltbie Babcock*

He is not great, who is not greatly good.

1975   *William Shakespeare*

I shall no longer ask myself if this or that is expedient, but only if it is right.

1968   *Alan Paton*

If one fights for good behavior, God makes one a present of good feelings.

1983   *Juliana Ewing*

Walk and talk and work and laugh with your friends, but behind the scenes, keep up the life of simple prayer and inward worship.

1981   *Thomas Kelly*

When you have written a wrathful letter - put it in the
  stove.

1953   *Abraham Lincoln*

The only safe and sure way to destroy an enemy is to
  make him your friend.

1953   *Anonymous*

The crimes that are now being committed by man
  against man cry aloud not for venegeance, but for
  a complete change in our relationship with one
  another.

1944   *George Lansbury*

Rejoice not when your enemy falls
Never exult when he is overthrown
If your enemy is hungry, give him food
And give him water if he thirsts
For so you shall quench blazing passions
And the Eternal will reward you.

1958   *Proverbs*

As one lamp lights another, nor grows less, so nobleness enkindleth nobleness.

1908   *Author Unknown*

Whene'er a noble deed is wrought
Whene'er is spoken a noble thought
Our hearts in glad surprise
To higher levels rise.

1939   *Henry W. Longfellow*

Teach us, good Lord, to serve Thee as Thou deserveth
To give and not to count the cost
To fight and not to heed the wounds
To toil and not to seek for rest
To labor and not to ask for any reward
Save that of knowing that we do Thy will.

1955   *Ignatius Loyola*

I listen with reverence to the bird song cascading at dawn from the oasis; for it seems to me there is no better evidence for the existence of God than in the bird that sings, though it knows not why, from a spring of untrammelled joy that wells up in its heart.

1965   *An Arab Chieftain*

O Lord, we thank thee for this universe, our great home. We praise Thee for the arching skies, and blessed winds; for the driving clouds, and the constellations on high. We praise Thee for the salt sea, and running water, for the everlasting hills, for the trees, and the grass under our feet.

Grant us a heart wide open to all this joy and beauty; and save our souls from being so steeped in care, or so darkened by passion that we pass heedless and unseeing when even the thornbush by the wayside is aflame with the glory of God.

1957   *Walter Rauschenbusch*

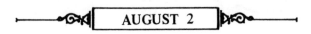

To love a man means to see him as God intended him
to be.

1960   *Hattingberg*

I believe, that despite so much wickedness and evil
design in the world, man is essentially good.

1973   *Ralph J. Bunche*

All men are redeemable, every man can be rehabili-
tated, and it is up to us in the community...to
see that this is done.

1973   *Benjamin Malcolm, New York City Corrections
Commissioner, 1972*

Let us strive to learn to live together.
Let us be patient with one another
And even patient with ourselves.
We have a long, long way to go
So let us hasten along the road
The road of man's tenderness and generosity.
Groping, we may find one another's hands in the
dark.

1973   *Emily Greene Balch*

I cannot see the life of Jesus as other than God trying
to disclose His love for us, and His attempt at any
price, to show us that the Cosmos is grounded in
love.

1967   *Douglas V. Steere*

"Blessed", says Jesus, "is the man who thinks lowly
of himself; who has passed through great trials;
who goes on and endures; who carries a tender
heart; who has a passion for holiness; who sweet-
ens human life; who dares to be true to conscience." What a conception of character!

1957   *John Watson*

However vast the tide of hate, the love of God is
unshakeable; and it is to unshakeable love man
is called.

1964   *Harold Loukes*

The good are always the merry.

1977   *St. Francis of Assisi*

All the world doth love the song that happy people
  sing.

1903   *Author Unknown*

The essence of humour is sensibility; warm, tender
  fellow-feeling with all forms of existence.

1984   *Thomas Carlyle*

A merry heart doeth good like a medicine.

1984   *Proverbs 17*

Look upon the rainbow, and praise Him that made it.

1983   *Ecclesiasticus*

To me who has been long in city pent
'Tis very sweet to look into the fair
And open face of heaven - to breathe a prayer
Full in the smile of the blue firmament.

1979   *John Keats*

Flower in the crannied wall
I pluck you out of the crannies
I hold you here, root and all, in my hand.
Little flower, but if I could understand
What you are, root and all, and all in all
I should know what God and man is.

1982   *Alfred, Lord Tennyson*

War! What is it after all the people get?
Why, taxes, widows, wooden legs and debt!

1917   *Author Unknown*

Though I have been trained as a soldier, and partici-
    pated in many battles, there never was a time
    when, in my opinion, some way could not have
    been found to prevent the drawing of the sword.

1915   *General Ulysses Grant*

I believe there is a heroism other than that which in-
    volves the inflicting of pain and death: a surer pro-
    tection for those I love than the slaughter of those
    someone else loves. With God's help, I will make
    the great adventure of faith, standing fearless, un-
    weaponed, save with the power of redemption.

1961   *T. Corder Catchpool*

It is not enough to try to prevent war; something
    must be done to remove its causes.

1938   *Sir Samuel Hoare*

Have a heart that never hardens
A temper that never tires
A touch that never hurts.

1975   *Charles Dickens*

If I can stop one heart from breaking,
I shall not live in vain
If I can ease one life the aching
Or cool one pain
Or help one fainting robin
Into his nest again
I shall not live in vain.

1964   *Emily Dickinson*

Everything becomes possible by the mere presence of
   someone who knows how to listen, to love and to
   give of himself.

1975   *Elie Wiesel*

Come now, little man! Flee for awhile from your
   tasks
Hide yourself for a little space from the turmoil of
   your thoughts
Come, cast aside your burdensome cares
And put aside your laborious pursuits
Give your time to God, and rest in Him for a little
   while.

1978   *St. Anselm of Canterbury*

Dazed with the noise and speed I run
And stay me on the changeless one
I stay myself on Him who stays
Ever the same through nights and days.

1968   *Katharine T. Hinkson*

For what must be I calmly wait
And trust the path I cannot see
That God is good sufficeth me.

1933   *John G. Whittier*

Prayer is the world in tune.

1977   *Henry Vaughan*

How much pain have we suffered, because of the evils
that never have happened.

1909   *Author Unknown*

If we dwell on life's hindrances, we may be blind to
its possibilities.

1917   *Author Unknown*

Better the storm with God, than the still waters without Him.

1980   *The Banner*

There is nothing too great for the Creator to accomplish, and nothing too small for Him to attend to.

1959   *The Rev. Henry Emerson Fosdick*

Fear thou not, for I am with thee.
Be not dismayed for I am thy God.
I will strengthen thee, yea I will help thee.

1911   *Isaiah*

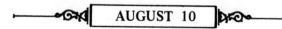

There is that by which all the world is pervaded.

1974   *The Bhagavad-Gita*

One does not doubt the existence of air because a
   strong wind is not always blowing, or of sunlight because night intervenes between dusk
   and dawn.

1964   *Aurobindo*

Mortal though I be, yea ephemeral, if but a moment
   I gaze up to the night's starry domain of heaven,
   then no longer on earth I stand. I touch the Creator, and my lively spirit drinketh immortality.

1982   *Ptolemy the Astronomer*

We thank Thee, our Father, for life and love; for the
   mystery and majesty of existence, and for the
   world of beauty which surrounds us.

1980   *Dr. Reinhold Niebuhr*

The road ahead may be veiled from sight, but you
must teach yourself to regard the unknown as
friendly.

1981 *Emmet Fox*

It is not God who is far away and dim
It is you and I who are far away from Him.

1952 *Pamela V. Starr*

In this life there is no end to the journey into the
mystery of God. That is why we continue to
grope our way as we seek Him out. He who
gropes for God will find Him.

1983 *Gerald Weiss*

Keep Thou my feet; I do not ask to see
The distant scene, one step enough for me.

1968 *John Henry Cardinal Newman*

God Himself is the country of the soul.

1977 *St. Augustine*

Keep me, my God! My boat is so small, and the
ocean is so wide.

1900   *Breton Fisherman's Prayer*

So long Thy power has blest me
Sure it still will lead me on.

1915   *Cardinal Newman*

Faith is not an easy virtue; but in the broad world of
man's voyage through time to eternity, faith is not
only a gracious companion, but an essential guide.

1984   *The Rev. Theodore Hesburgh*

The Lord thy God is with thee whithersoever thou
goest.

1981   *Joshua 1*

I am come that they might have life, and that they
    might have it more abundantly.

1973   *Jesus*

The wonder of the Christian gospel is that its mes-
    sage from God came through a life lived among
    men.   The gospel was not first read in a book.
    It was seen and known in Jesus.

1972   *The Rev. Walter Russell Bowie*

His presence was a peace to all
He bade the sorrowful rejoice
Pain turned to pleasure at His call
Health lived, and issued from His voice.
He healed the sick, and sent abroad
The dumb, rejoicing in the Lord
Yet He with trouble did remain
And suffered poverty and pain.

1972   *John Clare*

Lord Jesus Christ, Who are the Way, the Truth, and
    the Life
Suffer us not to stray from Thee, Who are the Way
Not to distrust Thee, Who art the Truth
Nor to rest in any other thing than Thee, Who are the
    Life.

1972   *Erasmus*

The follower of Jesus has to accept the role of living as responsibly as he can with the human dilemma, and leaving judgment and forgiveness in the hands of God.

1967   *Richard F. Hettlinger*

If you want to be a Good Samaritan today, you better stop the arms race; you better start a world food reserve; you better stop pollution.

That's what it means to be a Good Samaritan in the world to-day, because public issues so invade the privacy of every individual life that to deny them is to deny one's own humanity.

1977   *The Rev. William Sloane Coffin*

Nothing here below is profane for those who know how to see; on the contrary, everything is sacred.

1976   *Teilhard de Chardin*

Stand still, and consider the wondrous works of God.

1977   *Job*

I bind unto myself today
The virtues of the starlit heaven
The glorious sun's life-giving ray
The whiteness of the moon at even
The flashing of the lightning free
The whirling wind's tempestuous shock
The stable earth, the deep salt sea
Around the old eternal rocks.

1980   *from St. Patrick's Breastplate*

O Lord, our Savior, who hast warned that Thou
    wilt require much of those to whom much is
    given; grant that we, whose lot is cast in so
    goodly a heritage, may strive together the more
    abundantly to extend to others what we so
    richly enjoy.

1979   *St. Augustine*

Love is the goal
Love is the way we wend.

1963   *Christina Rossetti*

Love means taking up other lives into our own.

1958   *Anonymous*

Those who go forth ministering to the wants and
   necessities of their fellow beings experience a
   rich return, their souls being as a watered garden,
   and a spring that faileth not.

1981   *Lucretia Mott*

For, as God's love is universal, so when the mind is
   sufficiently influenced by it, it begets a likeness of
   itself, and the heart is enlarged toward all men.

1982   *John Woolman*

To be of use in the world is the only way to be
    happy.

1922

Hans Christian Andersen

Happiness...is attained through fidelity to a worthy
    purpose.

1948

Helen Keller

A sense of humor will reduce your troubles to their
    proper proportion.

1949

Author Unknown

The heart that is truly happy never grows old.

1939

Author Unknown

God made you
God loves you
God keeps you.

1898

Author Unknown

I would not live without the love of my friends.

1941   *John Keats*

A friend is one who knows all about you and still likes you.

1951   *George F. Hoffman*

Cultivate the habit of always seeing the best in people.

1941   *Theodore Cuyler*

The sacrifice of love, the generous giving
When friends were few, the handshake warm and
    strong
The fragrance of each life of holy living
Let us remember long.

1905   *Author Unknown*

I know that if I offer my friendship to all as Christ
    did, I shall begin to feel the cosmic love which is
    God.

1982   *Paramahansa Yogananda*

Almost all men improve upon acquaintance.

1950   *André Maurois*

If we could read the secret history of our enemies, we
    should find in each man's life sorrow and suffering
    enough to disarm all hostility.

1939   *Author Unknown*

We are now trying to understand people who are dif-
    ferent instead of shooting people who are differ-
    ent.

1962   *Danilo Dolci*

There is a spirit abroad in life...
That makes for wholenness and for community
It broods over the demonstrations for justice
And brings comfort to the desolate and forgotten
Who have no memory of what it is to feel
The rhythm of belonging...
It knows no country, and its allies are to be found
Wherever the heart is kind.

1976   *The Rev. Howard Thurman*

Know ye not that ye are the temple of God, and that the spirit of God dwelleth within you?

1966   *St. Paul*

The serene, silent beauty of a holy life is the most powerful influence in the world, next to the might of God.

1917   *Blaise Pascal*

Glory be to Thee, O Lord, for the laughter of children, for mirth and wit, for the jest of the gallant souls that make us ashamed to be afraid, and for the cheerfulness of suffering folk, who shame us out of self-concern...Make us to know Thee aright, and to enjoy and possess Thee more and more.

1980   *St. Anselm*

Be not over-eager after outward things, but keep above them in the Lord's power.

1952   *George Fox*

True simplicity consists not in the use of particular forms, but in foregoing over-indulgence, in maintaining humility of spirit, in keeping the material surroundings of our lives directly serviceable to necessary ends, even though these surroundings may properly be characterized by grace, symmetry and beauty.

1981   *Book of Discipline, Society of Friends*

Make generosity the law of your life.

1978   *W. N. Clarke*

Pray God, keep us simple.

1965   *William Thackeray*

Whoe'er feels deeply, feels for all who live.

1984

Madame de Staël

And there are those who give, and know not pain
    in giving, nor do they seek joy, nor give with
    mindfulness of virtue.

They give, as in yonder valley, the myrtle breathes
    its fragrance into space.

Through the hands of such as these, God speaks, and
    from behind their eyes, He smiles upon the earth.

1984

Kahlil Gibran

Every noble life leaves the fibre of it interwoven for-
    ever in the work of the world.

1932

John Ruskin

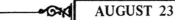
Teach us to build, O Master, until Thy kingdom come.

1941   *Hornell Hart*

When I lie down worn out, other men will stand
    young, fresh.
By the steps that I have cut, they will climb.
By the stairs that I have built, they will mount.
They will never know the name of the man who made
    them.
At the clumsy work they will laugh
When the stones roll, they will curse me,
But they will mount, and on my work
They will climb, and on my stairs.

1965   *Olive Schreiner*

No difficulties, no discovery!

1942   *The Rev. Joseph Fort Newton*

A tree that takes both arms to encircle grew from a
    tiny rootlet
A many-storied pagoda is built by placing one brick
    upon another brick
A journey of three thousand miles is begun by a sin-
    gle step.

1963   *Lao Tzu*

So here hath been dawning
Another blue day
Think! Wilt thou let it
Slip useless away?

Out of eternity
This new day is born
Into eternity
At night will return.

1898   *Thomas Carlyle*

Be ashamed to die until you have won some victory
    for humanity.

1948   *Horace Mann*

Our hope is in heroic men
Star-led to build the world again.

1982   *Edwin Markham*

Out of the shadows of night
The world rolls into light
It is daybreak everywhere!

1905   *Last words from Longfellow's pen*

Every particular thou, is a glimpse through to the
eternal Thou.

1983   *Martin Buber*

Do not go wrathfully
Nor with appraising eye;
The world is far too dear,
Too swift, to cloud its poignancy.
So little serves to break
The cords of tenderness;
We are too close to death
To chide one another.

Do not draw down regret
Upon the fragile day;
Even a sigh can halt
Its life which flows so trustingly.
What comes is too beloved,
No change can be for good;
We have no time but now
To cherish one another.

1960   *Winifred Rawlins*

Love keeps no score of wrongs.

1967   *1 Corinthians (New English Bible)*

One fire is not quenched by another fire, but by
water.

1967   *St. John Chrysosthom*

There is a spirit which I feel that delights to do no
evil, nor to revenge any wrong. If it is betrayed,
it bears it, for its ground and spring are the mercies and forgiveness of God. Its crown is meek-
ness; its life, everlasting love unfeigned. It takes
its kingdom with entreaty, and not with con-
tention. In God alone it can rejoice.

1956   *James Nayler*

Praised be my Lord for all those who pardon one
another for His love's sake, and who endure weakness and tribulation. Blessed are they who peace-
ably shall endure, for Thou, O Most High, shall
give them a crown.

1979   *St. Francis of Assisi*

The best way to know God is to love many things.

1970   *Vincent van Gogh*

What's the earth
With all its art, verse, music worth -
Compared with love, found, gained and kept?

1967   *Robert Browning*

Love is enough though the world be a-waning.

1970   *William Morris*

Not where I breathe, but where I love, I live.

1977   *Robert Southwell*

Love is always an active concern for the growth and
    aliveness of the one we love.

1970   *Erich Fromm*

The sword is always conquered by the spirit.

1943   *Napoleon*

There is more force in a touch than in a blow.

1913   *Author Unknown*

Let there be peace on earth, and let it begin with me.
Let there be peace on earth, the peace that was meant
   to be.
With God as our Father, brothers all are we
Let me walk with my brother, in perfect harmony.

1967   *American Folksong*

Love always leads to the truth about men, more surely than logic.

1981   *Sir Wilfred Grenfell*

Fair is the sunshine, fairer still the moonlight
And all the twinkling, starry host
Jesus shines brighter, Jesus shines fairer
Than all the angels heaven can boast.

1955   *Crusaders' Hymn*

O, God of mountains, stars and boundless spaces
O, God of freedom, and of joyous hearts
When Thy face looketh forth from all men's faces
There will be room enough in crowded marts!
Brood Thou around me, and the noise is o'er
Thy universe my closet with shut door.

1965   *George MacDonald*

The earth is full of the loving kindness of the Lord.

1962   *Psalms*

For all that has been - thanks!
For all that shall be - yes!

1966
                                    Dag Hammarskjöld

There is one supreme virtue a man may have; it is
    loyalty to the adventure of life.

1966
                                    Arthur E. Morgan

Make us Thy mountaineers
We would not linger on the lower slope
Fill us afresh with hope, O God of hope
That undefeated we may climb the hill.

1962
                                    Amy Carmichael

I will instruct thee and teach thee in the way which
    thou shalt go.

1947
                                    Psalm 32

There is no solace on the earth for us - for such as
   we -
Who search for the hidden city that eyes may never
   see
Only the road and the dawn, the sun, the wind, and
   the rain
And the watch-fire under the stars, and sleep, and the
   road again
We travel the dusty road till the light of the day is
   dim
And sunset shows us spires away on the world's rim
We travel from dawn to dusk till the day is past and
   by
Seeking the Holy City beyond the rim of the sky.

1968   *John Masefield*
                              (Abridged from "The Seekers")

Religion is born when we accept the ultimate frustra-
   tion of mere human effort, and at the same time
   realize the strength which comes from union with
   superhuman reality.

1968   *John Buchan*

No man is born into the world whose work is not born with him.

1914   *James R. Lowell*

To work for the common good is the greatest creed.

1970   *Dr. Albert Einstein*

No ray of sunlight is ever lost, but the green which it awakens into existence needs time to sprout, and it is not always granted to the sower to see the harvest. All work that is worth anything is done in faith.

1964   *Dr. Albert Schweitzer*

Grant that I may always desire more than I can accomplish.

1971   *Michelangelo*

Honest toil is holy service.

1936   *The Rev. Henry van Dyke*

The dignity of labor depends not on what you do,
but how you do it.

1924   *Edwin Grover*

We shall prosper in proportion as we learn to dignify
and glorify labor, and put brains and skill into the
common occupations of life.

1943   *Booker T. Washington*

Life is enlarged in an amazing way as we pour out our
best.

1972   *Friends Yearly Meeting Epistle*

Be strong and work, for I am with you, saith the
Lord.

1915   *Haggai 2*

SEPTEMBER 3

Every failure teaches a man something, if he will
    listen.

1914   *Charles Dickens*

He that well and rightly considereth his own work
    will find little cause to judge badly of another.

1967   *Thomas à Kempis*

The heights by great men reached and kept
Were not attained by sudden flight
But they, while their companions slept
Were toiling upward in the night.

1909   *Henry W. Longfellow*

God, give me work
'Till my life shall end
And life
Till my work is done.

1965   *Winifred Holtby*

I am still learning.

1953   *Michelangelo's Motto*

Our life is really a long process of education, in find-
    ing an order of values and choosing what is best
    and truest for us.

1963   *Stephen F. Bayne*

The disciplined use of the mind becomes an ethical
    obligation.

1963   *Edwin E. Aubrey*

Education to-day has an all-important task: develop
    a new man, who is not indifferent to the needs of
    his brother.

1962   *Oliver Caldwell*

Minds are needed now more than ever before, provid-
    ed they are the products of warm hearts.

1976   *The Rev. William Sloane Coffin, Jr.*

Education is to create men who can:

> See clearly
> Imagine vividly
> Think steadily
> And will nobly.

1976   *Edward Leen*

If maturity can be defined as caring intelligently
for other people, then anyone who can act
sensitively and considerately most of the time
is mature.   To help children grow into really
mature people, is perhaps the major goal of
a school.

1971   *Henry Scattergood*

The one you influence to-day may grow up to influence a hundred thousand people.

1967   *A Youth Worker*

O God, who hast sent us to school in this strange life
of ours, and hast set us tasks which test all our
courage, trust and fidelity, may we not spend our
days complaining at circumstance, or fretting at
discipline, but give ourselves to learn of life.

1973   *W. E. Orchard*

Live your life while you have it. Life is a splendid gift; there is nothing small about it; but to live your life, you must discipline it.

1939   *Florence Nightingale*

Chance favors the prepared mind.

1963   *Louis Pasteur*

In times like these, we do not need to educate our children to have all qualities we think are necessary. Rather, we have to educate our children to be...flexible, innovative, and for our crowding world, strong enough to love and co-operate with one another.

1976   *Thomas Scattergood*

Perhaps the most valuable result of all education is the ability to make ourselves do the thing we have to do, when it ought to be done, whether we like it or not.

1953   *Author Unknown*

A loving heart is the truest wisdom.

1980

Charles Dickens

When you love someone, you love him as he is.

1957

Charles Péguy

Love is a state of mind which considers the well
being of others as important as that of his own.

1965

W. Stuart Nelson

God weigheth more with how much love a man work-
eth, than how much he doeth. He doeth much
that loveth much. He doeth much that doeth a
thing well.

1983

Thomas à Kempis

Whoever rightly advocates the cause of some, thereby
   promotes the good of all.

1972   *John Woolman*

I believe that an individual's greatest pride, as well as
   his greatest contribution to society, may lie in the
   ways in which he is different from me and others,
   rather than in the way he conforms to the crowd.
   I shall therefore accept the differences, and endeavor to build a useful relationship upon them.

1984   *Linton B. Swift*

All men are brothers, loved of God - the churched,
   the unchurched; the wicked, the saintly.

1983   *Pope John XXIII*

As far as possible, without surrender, be on good terms with all persons. Speak your truth quietly and clearly; and listen to others, even the dull and the ignorant. They, too, have their story. Do not be cynical about love; for in the face of all aridity and disenchantment, it is as perennial as the grass.

1968   *from Desiderata*

Let no man think to have set his own house in order, if he is unmindful of his brother's well-being.

1960   *St. John Chrysostom*

To each of us, God will be asking just one question: "How did you treat your fellow man?"

1971   *The Most Rev. Terence J. Cooke*

I sought my soul
But my soul I could not see
I sought my God
But my God eluded me
I sought my brother
And I found all three.

1962   *Author Unknown*

A man wrapped up in himself makes a very small
    bundle.

1951   *Benjamin Franklin*

It is when we forget ourselves that we do things that
    are remembered.

1917   *Author Unknown*

The best portion of a good man's life
His little, nameless, unremembered acts of kindness
    and of love.

1915   *William Wordsworth*

My power is faint and low, till I have learned to serve.

1966   *George Matheson*

The actions of men are the best interpreters of their
    thoughts.

1941   *John Locke*

Spend as much time as you can with the trees and
 birds and flowers.

1904   *Author Unknown*

To see a world in a grain of sand
And heaven in a wild flower
Hold infinity in the palm of your hand
And eternity in an hour.

1973   *William Blake*

Small flowers there are beside the stoniest way,
And on the seeming-endless journeying,
Some breaths of air are sweet, and some birds sing
And some new goal is reached in every day.

1965   *Kenneth Boulding*

A handful of pine seed will cover mountains with the
 green majesty of forest. I, too, will set my face to
 the wind, and throw my handful of seed on high.

1972   *William Sharp*

This is the day the Lord hath made.
We will rejoice and be glad in it.

1984   *Psalm 118*

Listen to the exhortation of the dawn!
Look to this day! For it is life,
        The very life of life.
In its brief course lie all the verities
And realities of your existence,
        The bliss of growth
        The glory of action
        The splendor of beauty;
For yesterday is but a dream,
And tomorrow is only a vision,
        But to-day well lived
Makes every yesterday a dream of happiness
And every tomorrow a vision of hope.
Look well, therefore, to this day!
Such is the salutation of the dawn.

1967   *From the Sanskrit*

The day shall not be up so soon as I
To try the fair adventure of tomorrow.

1972

William Shakespeare

Any man can be as big as he wants. No problem of
human destiny is beyond human beings. Man's
reason and spirit have often solved the seemingly
insolvable - and we believe they can do it again.

1964

John F. Kennedy

I ought, therefore I can.

1964

Immanuel Kant

The image of every true act, the strength of every
true feeling, belong to eternity.

1971

Herman Hesse

Yesterday cannot be recalled
Tomorrow cannot be assured
To-day only is thine.

1897   *Author Unknown*

Time, indeed is a sacred gift;
each day is a little life.

1917   *Sir John Lubbock*

Life can only be understood backwards,
but it can only be lived forwards.

1970   *Søren Kierkegaard*

To everything there is a season, and a time for every
    purpose under heaven.

1969   *Ecclestiastes*

You can move back, or you can move on, but you
cannot stand still.

1976

Sir Robert Peel

Why are we melancholy?   Sometimes it is because
we are selfish.

1980

Author Unknown

If your morals make you dreary, depend on it, they
are wrong.

1980

Robert L. Stevenson

You can only make men free if they are inwardly
bound by their own sense of responsibility.

1964

William Ernest Hocking

Those love truth best who to themselves are true
And what they dare to dream of, dare to do.

1916

James R. Lowell

Look thou within
Within thee is the fountain of good
And it will ever spring
If thou wilt ever delve.

1959   *Marcus Aurelius*

A humble knowledge of thyself is a surer way to God
    than a deep search after learning. Yet learning is
    not to be blamed, for that is good in itself, and or-
    dained by God; but a good conscience and a virtu-
    ous life are always to be preferred before it. He is
    truly learned that doeth the will of God.

1960   *Thomas à Kempis*

Our Father, help us to act on the bit of truth that we
    know.

1972   *Jane Saddler*

Mirth is like a flash of lightening. Cheerfulness keeps
   up a kind of daylight in the mind.

1947   *Joseph Addison*

Those who want happiness must stoop to find it. It is
   a flower that grows in every vale.

1966   *William Blake*

Praise God that thou art called to share
The task of making all things fair
'Till health and gladness, joy and mirth
Shall spring like flowers, o'er all the earth.

1963   *F. J. Gillman*

The joy of the Lord is your strength.

1965   *Nehemiah*

The wind of God is always blowing, but I must hoist my sails.

1956   *Author Unknown*

To hope means to be ready at every moment for that which is not yet born, and yet not become desperate if there is no birth in our lifetime. Those whose hope is weak settle down for comfort or violence; those whose hope is strong see and cherish all signs of new life, and are ready at every moment to help the birth of that which is ready to be born.

1972   *Eric Fromm*

All right use of life...is to pave ways for the firmer footing of those who succeed us.

1912   *George Meredith*

I need to know how good can be strong enough to
    break out of the possessive arms of evil. Where
    shall I look for triumph? Somewhere, not be-
    yond our scope is a Power, participating but un-
    harnessed, waiting to be led toward us. Good has
    a singular strength not known to evil.

1968   *Christopher Fry*

I believe that God will give us all the strength we
    need, to help us resist in all times of distress; but
    he never gives it in advance, lest we should rely on
    ourselves, and not on Him alone.

1981   *Dietrich Bonhoeffer*

Faith is a bird that feels the light, and sings while
    the dawn is still dark.

1966   *Sir Rabindranath Tagore*

The man who most truly can be accounted brave is he who most knows the meaning of what is sweet in life, and what is terrible, and then goes out undeterred to meet what is to come.

1975   *Socrates*

I believe it is the quiet rebel, the men and women of conscience, standing courageously alone and peacefully affirming, at whatever cost, the truth as they see it, who have lifted humanity out of barbarism.

1975   *Stephen G. Cary*

If there be in front of us any painful duty, strengthen us with the grace of courage; if any act of mercy, teach us tenderness and patience.

1914   *Robert L. Stevenson*

Everyone needs a friend. Be sure to be one to somebody; and remember always that God sent Christ
into the world to be the friend of every man.

1915   *Slattery*

He took our common life, and daily toil, and turned
them into divine things.

1960   *Friends Book of Discipline*

Jesus Christ was born to show forth the perfect life,
which puts love before all else - a love which is
available to all, and which, by its nature of self-
sacrifice, can overcome evil.

1960   *Eric Tucker*

The best gift a man can make to mankind, is his best
self.

1924   *Author Unknown*

I sing a song of the saints of God,
Patient and brave and true
Who toiled and fought and lived and died
For the Lord they loved and knew
And one was a doctor and one was a queen
And one was a shepherdess on the green
They were all of them saints of God
And I mean, God helping, to be one, too.

They lived not only in ages past
There are hundreds of thousands still
The world is bright with joyous saints
Who love to do Jesus' will.
You can meet them in school, or in lanes, or at sea
In church, or in trains, or in shops, or at tea
For the saints of God are just folks like me.
And I mean to be one, too.

1963   *L. Scott*

The distinctive mark of a saint, is that he makes it
    easier to believe in God.

1963   *T. R. GLover*

Every real communion with God is inevitably linked
   up with a new relatedness to our neighbor.

1966   *Canon Raven*

Who works for justice works with Thee
Who works in love, Thy child shall be.

1962   *The Rev. Samuel Longfellow*

When we clothe the naked
 Feed the hungry
Comfort the distressed
   (Anyone, anywhere)
We do it unto him.

1967   *Lorraine Calhoun*

He prayeth best, who loveth best
All things, both great and small
For the dear God who loveth us
He made and loveth all.

1893   *S. T. Coleridge*

When thou would'st cheer thine heart, think upon the good qualities of thy associates.

1967   *Marcus Aurelius*

A man who desires to help others by counsel or deed, will refrain from dwelling on men's faults, and will speak but sparingly of human weaknesses.

1967   *Benedict de Spinoza*

Life is not so short, but there is always time enough for courtesy.

1914   *Ralph W. Emerson*

There is a wonderful power in kind words.

1887   *Author Unknown*

The earth is full of the grandeur of God.

1966   *Gerard Manley Hopkins*

The grand essentials to happiness in this life are something to do, something to love, and something to hope for.

1971   *Joseph Addison*

Gather the crumbs of happiness, and they will make you a loaf of contentment.

1975   *Author Unknown*

These are the gifts I ask of Thee, Spirit Serene
Strength for the daily task
Courage to face the road
Good cheer to help me bear the traveller's load
And for the hours of rest that come between
An inward joy in all things heard and seen.

1932   *Rev. Henry van Dyke*

True and solid peace of nations consists not in equality of arms, but in mutual trust alone.

1964

Pope John XXIII

I have an unfaltering faith in human nature, and seek no protection but that which God wills for those who trust Him. This is my understanding of Christ's way of life, a practical way both for individuals and for nations. Someday a nation will have the courage to disarm and put these convictions to the test; and I have absolute confidence in the issue.

1979

T. Corder Catchpool

The only sure weapon against bad ideas, is better ideas.

1964

S. Whitney Griswold

Be it yours to evolve the life of your country in loveliness and strength.

1967

Joseph Mazzini

If anything is clear from the Gospel, it is that knowing the evil that was in the world and in the heart
of man, Christ yet retained his unbounded faith
that goodness would in the end prevail.

1978   *The Rev. C. F. Andrews*

Commit thy way to Jesus, thy burdens and thy cares
He from them all releases, He all thy sorrow shares.
He gives the winds their courses, and bounds the
    ocean's shores.
He suffers not temptation to rise beyond thy power.

1970   *St. Matthew Passion - J. S. Bach*

An infinite love directs
The destiny of your life and mine.

1908   *Author Unknown*

Prayer is the serious, thoughtful, persistent endeavor
    to put our lives at the service of the best.

1974   *Frederick M. Eliot*

God keeps up a continual conversation with every
    human creature.

1974   *Paul Claudel*

He who lives a life of good, and charity, is constantly
    at worship.

1966   *Emmanuel Swedenborg*

Teach me, my God and King
In all things Thee to see
And what I do in anything
To do it as for Thee.

1905   *George Herbert*

Power over life must be balanced by reverence for
life.

1970   *Anne M. Lindbergh*

Man's great troubles are man-created; and intelligence
and love linked together, are strong enough to triumph.

1970   *Lewis M. Stevens*

You cannot control the events of your life, but you
can control your reaction to these events.

1971   *The Rev. Howard Thurman*

No matter how cruel an era, or bleak the times, true
heroes arrive in it. They may or may not be religious believers, but their existences follow the
Gospel pattern. They comfort the afflicted, give
to the poor, turn the other cheek, remain cheerful
in adversity, lay down their lives for a friend.

1971   *Phyllis McGinley*

The time is past when good men can remain silent.

1972   *Daniel Berrigan, S.J.*

The true worth of a man is to be measured by the
objects he pursues.

1935   *Marcus Aurelius*

I asked God for strength, that I might achieve.
I was made weak, that I might learn humbly to obey.
I asked for power, that I might have the praise of
men.
I was given weakness, that I might feel the need of
God.
I asked for all things that I might enjoy life.
I was given life, that I might enjoy all things.

1961   *An Unknown Confederate Soldier*

Behold, the Kingdom of God is within you.

1929   *St. Luke*

Then came October, full of merry glee.

1980   *Edmund Spenser*

To make this earth our hermitage
A cheerful and a changeful place
God's bright and intricate device
Of days and seasons doth suffice.

1979   *Robert L. Stevenson*

Our Creator would never have made such lovely days,
    and given us the deep hearts to enjoy them, unless
    we were meant to be immortal.

1962   *Nathaniel Hawthorne*

The heavens declare the glory of God, and the firma-
    ment showeth his handiwork.

1956   *Psalm 19*

The earth is the Lord's, and the fullness thereof;
   the world, and they that dwell therein.

1972   *Psalm 14*

Shall we not learn from life, its laws, dynamics, bal-
   ances?
Learn to base our needs not on death, destruction,
   waste, but on renewal?
In wisdom and in gentleness learn to walk again with
   Eden's angels?
Learn at last to shape a civilization in harmony with
   the earth? ...

... This, as citizens, we all inherit; this, ours to love
   and live upon, and use wisely down all the
   generations of the future.

1972   *from This Is The American Earth*
                            Ansel Adams and Nancy Newhall

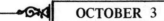

Stand still, and consider the wondrous works of God.

1977   *Job*

Never lose an opportunity of seeing anything that is
    beautiful, for beauty is God's handwriting - a way-
    side sacrament.   Welcome it in every fair face, in
    every fair sky, in every flower, and thank God for
    it as a cup of blessing.

1971   *Ralph W. Emerson*

Be still, my heart. These great trees are prayers.

1977   *Rabindranath Tagore*

Everything that lives is holy.
Life delights in life.

1978   *William Blake*

We are God's fellow-workers.

1964   *1 Corinthians*

We cannot do everything at once, but we can do
    something at once.

1927   *A. C. Coolidge*

Do well the little things now; so shall great things
    come to thee by and by, asking to be done.

1919   *Persian Proverb*

If there be lying before you any bit of work from
    which you shrink, go straight to it. The only way
    to get rid of it is to do it.

1927   *Alexander MacLaren*

Act well at the moment, and you have performed a
    good·action to all eternity.

1935   *The Rev. Johann Lavater*

Let gentle words soothe woe and pain.
We shall not pass this way again.

1892   *Author Unknown*

To cultivate kindness is a great part of the business
    of life.

1923   *Samuel Johnson*

Sympathy is the safeguard of the soul against selfish-
    ness.

1939   *Thomas Carlyle*

The best kind of sympathy is that which lends a
    hand.

1912   *Author Unknown*

Bear ye one another's burdens, and so fulfill the law
    of Christ.

1914   *St. Paul*

In God have I put my trust; I will not be afraid.

1928   *Psalm 56*

Let nothing disturb thee
Nothing affright thee
All things are passing
God never changeth
Patient endurance
Attaineth to all things
Who God possesseth
In nothing is wanting
Alone God sufficeth.

1982   *St. Teresa's Book Mark*
                                          (Longfellow translation)

Oh, how great peace and quietness would he possess
   who should cut off all vain anxiety, and place all
   his confidence in God.

1982   *Thomas à Kempis*

The dear Lord's best interpreters
Are humble human souls.

1942   *John G. Whittier*

We are very blessed that is the meek who are to inherit the earth, for they can be trusted with it.

1981   *Madeleine L'Engle*

Christianity's fundamental tenet is, as I see it, a belief
that self-sacrificing love is both the best and most
powerful of all the spiritual impulses that are
known to us.

1971   *Arnold Toynbee*

Always decide to use humble love. If you resolve on
that, once for all, you may subdue the whole
world.

1974   *Feodor Dostoevski*

He hath said, "I will never leave thee, nor forsake thee."

1971   *Hebrews*

It is necessary, while in darkness, to know that there is a light somewhere; to know that in oneself, waiting to be found, there is a light.

1969   *James Baldwin*

When our hearts are wintry,
grieving or in pain
Thy touch can call us back
to life again.

1971   *J. M. C. Crum*

In the great quiet of God
My troubles are but the pebbles on the road.
My joys are like the everlasting hills.

1969   *Walter Rauschenbusch*

I look not at tongue and speech
I look at the spirit and the inward feeling
I look into the heart to see whether it be lovely.

1968   *Jalalu'ddin Rumi*

Whatsoever things are true
Whatsoever things are honest
Whatsoever things are lovely
Whatsoever things are of good report
If there be any virtue, and if there be any praise
Think on these things.

1978   *St. Paul (Philippians)*

Who shares his life's pure pleasures
And walks the honest road
Who trades with heaping measures
And lifts his brother's load
Who turns the wrong down bluntly
And lends the right a hand
He dwells in God's own country
He tills the Holy Land.

1958   *The Rev. Louis F. Benson*

My interest is in the future, because I am going to spend the rest of my life there.

1950   *Charles F. Kettering*

We are rising to the conviction that we are part of nature, and so a part of God; that the whole creation...is travelling together toward some great end; and that now, after ages of development, we have at length become conscious portions of the great scheme, and can co-operate in it with knowledge, and with joy. We are no aliens in a strange universe. We are parts of a developing whole, all enfolded in an embracing and interpenetrating love, of which we too...sometimes experience the joy too deep for words.

1984   *Sir Oliver Lodge*

Be still and know that I am God.

1969   *Psalm 46*

We bow unto the Light Divine that burns within
every living soul.

1969   *Hindu Chant*

The vocation of every man and woman is to serve
other people.

1970   *Leo Tolstoy*

We will not put national barriers around human need.

1973   *American Friends Service Committee*

Life is short
And we have not too much time for gladdening
The hearts of those who are travelling the dark way
with us.
Oh, be swift to love! Make haste to be kind!

1971   *Henri-Frédéric Amiel*

God is always nearer, mightier, more loving, and more free to help every one of us, than any of us ever realizes.

1967   *D. S. Cairns*

I feel the winds of God to-day
To-day my sail I lift
Though heavy oft with drenching spray
And torn with many a rift.
If hope but light the water's crest
And Christ my barque will use
I'll seek the seas at his behest
And dare another cruise.

1955   *Author Unknown*

Wheresoever I go, Thou art my companion.
Thou takest me by the hand and guideth me.

1965   *Tukaram*

OCTOBER 13

He loves both more than you, and before you love at
all.   .

1967   *Bernard of Clairvaux*

O God, I need Thee
When morning crowds the night away
And tasks of waking seize my mind
I need Thy poise.
When clashes come with those
Who walk the way with me
I need Thy smile.
When love is hard to see
Amid the ugliness and slime
I need Thy eyes.
When the path to take before me
Lies - I see it - courage flees
I need Thy faith.
When the day's work is done
Tired, discouraged, wasted
I need Thy rest.

1966   *The Rev. Howard Thurman*

Let not your heart be troubled, neither let it be
afraid.

1969   *St. John*

We are His workmanship.

1964   *Ephesians*

Remember you hold your body and your nervous sys-
    tem in trust from God, and must treat His prop-
    erty well.

1964   *Evelyn Underhill*

Be gentle with yourself. You are a child of the Uni-
    verse, no less that the trees and the stars. You
    have a right to be here, and whether or not it is
    clear to you, no doubt the Universe is unfolding
    as it should.

1967   *from Desiderata*

Come unto Me, all ye that labor and are heavy laden,
    and I will give you rest.

1968   *St. Matthew*

Problems are only opportunities in work clothes.

1959   *Henry J. Kaiser*

The greater the difficulty, the more glory in sur-
    mounting it. Skillful pilots gain their reputations
    from storms and tempests.

1920   *Epicurus*

We can keep going, if by God's power
We only bear the burdens of the hour.

1902   *Author Unknown*

The way to make the best of any situation is to make
    it better.

1914   *H. F. Cope*

It is better to light a candle than to curse the dark-
    ness.

1943   *Old Chinese Proverb*

Work is love made visible.

1954   *Kahlil Gibran*

Every individual has a place to fill in the world,
    and is important in some respect, whether he
    chooses to be so or not.

1984   *Nathaniel Hawthorne*

This learned I from the shadow of a tree
Which to and fro did sway against a wall
Our shadow selves -- our influence -- may fall
Where we ourselves can never be.

1960   *Anna E. Hamilton*

What can one person do?   Who can tell, in God's
    calculations?

1983   *Dorothy Steere*

Joy is the strength of the people of God.

1965
J. Rendel Harris

How good is man's life, the mere living!
How fit to employ
All the heart and the soul and the senses
Forever in joy!

1964
Robert Browning

He that is of a merry heart hath a continual feast.

1960
Proverbs

Good Lord, give us a heart for simple things - love,
laughter, bread and wine, dreams and still more
dreams.

1980
Author Unknown

Ever in the strife with your own thoughts, obey the
   nobler instinct.

1928   *Ralph W. Emerson*

Naught shall affright us, on Thy goodness leaning
Low in the heart faith singeth still her song
Chastened by pain, we learn life's deeper meaning
And in our weakness Thou dost make us strong.

1918   *The Rev. F. L. Hosmer*

If, in any measure, you have it in your choice,
Then it is a great and urgent duty to be glad and to
   be strong.

1960   *John Kelman*

God does not demand impossibilities.

1922   *St. Augustine*

Our destiny as a great nation depends directly on what you and I are like. The place to begin is with yourself. The time to begin is now.

1966   *F. N. D. Buchman*

I believe it is necessary to have a strong conviction that life has meaning, and that what I do with it matters.

1970   *William D. Lotspeich*

Some men see things as they are, and say, "Why?" I dream of things that never were, and say, "Why not?"

1970   *Robert F. Kennedy*

I am not the champion of lost causes, but the champion of causes not yet won.

1976   *Norman Thomas*

The light which shows us our sin, is the light that heals us.

1970

George Fox

Redemption does not deny the event of the wrong. But the Christian meaning of a fresh start is that we can be saved from the results of everything that has made our lives mean, dirty, and miserable -- by the stirring of our inner life, and by acceptance of God's pardon.

1970

Lewis M. Stevens

Past failures are guideposts for future success.

1953

Nicholas Biddle

God is so high you can't get above Him
God is so low you can't get beneath Him
God is so wide you can't get around Him
You'd better come in by the gate.

1957

Old Negro Spiritual

Judge not thy neighbor until thou find thyself in his position.

1909   *Author Unknown*

By others' faults, wise men correct their own.

1910   *Author Unknown*

No man is free who is not master of himself.

1926   *Epictetus*

Self-mastery is the essence of heroism.

1920   *Ralph W. Emerson*

O God, eternal and ever blessed, order what is disordered in our lives. Bring our minds to Thy truth, our conscience to Thy law, and our hearts to Thy love.

1958   *Prayer of the Church of Scotland*

Jesus knelt to share with Thee
The silence of eternity
Interpreted by love.

1983   *John G. Whittier*

Never forget that life is nothing but a growing in
    love, and a preparation for eternity.

1969   *Christoph Probst*

Life, I repeat, is energy of love, Divine or human
Exercised in pain, in strife and tribulation
And ordained, if so approved and sanctified
To pass through shades and silent rest
To endless joy.

1969   *William Wordsworth*

I, a pilgrim of eternity, stand before Thee, O Eternal
    One. Make me wise to see all things under the
    form of eternity, and make me brave enough to
    face all the changes in my life such a vision may
    entail.

1970   *John Baillie*

Divine love always has met, and always will meet
    every human need.

1970
                                    Mary Baker Eddy

Life is meant to be lived from a Center, a Divine Cen-
    ter. The deepest need of man is not food, cloth-
    ing and shelter, important as they are; it is God.

1981
                                        Thomas Kelly

In heavenly love abiding, no change my heart shall
    fear
And safe is such confiding, for nothing changes here.
The storms may roar without me, my heart may low
    be laid
But God is round about me, and can I be dismayed?

1973
                                    Anna L. Waring

This, then, is faith: God, felt by the heart.

1984
                                      Blaise Pascal

In every man there is something that is not of dust or
flesh, but of God.

1967   *George Fox*

I am convinced that the universe is under the control
of a loving purpose, and that in the struggle for
righteousness man has cosmic companionship.

1969   *The Rev. Martin Luther King, Jr.*

While the old order is destroying itself, a new order
of men and nations has already begun its slow but
sure evolution:

        Its name is Brotherhood
        Its method is Co-operation
        And its spirit is Love.

1975   *Mackenzie King*

Call unto Me, and I will answer thee, and show thee
great and mighty things thou knowest not.

1944   *Jeremiah 33*

The struggle between faith and fear will decide the destiny of our nation.

1975

Adlai Stevenson

Our precious little planet is in perhaps the most critical stage of its whole existence. It is in a position of immense danger and immense potentiality.

1981

Kenneth Boulding

A man's feet should be planted in his country, but his eyes should survey the world.

1984

George Santayana

All things are possible once enough human beings realize that the whole of the human future is at stake.

1983

Norman Cousins

Beware, when the great God lets loose a thinker on this planet!

1984

Ralph W. Emerson

Justice is the moral imperative of our time.

1976   *The Rev. William Sloane Coffin, Jr.*

Conflicts continue to exist clearly, and must not be
    masked...but with our weak powers we can help
    relieve the tension evoked by conflicts, if we seek
    to fulfill at the same time both of Jesus' com-
    mandments: the commandment of love, and the
    commandment of truth.

1983   *Margarethe Lachmund*

What is our hope? It is the triumph of righteousness
    in my own country. I am not prepared to stop
    working for these things just because change is
    dangerous. I believe the denial of change to be
    more dangerous.

1977   *Alan Paton of South Africa*

Part of my mission given, I believe, by God, is to
    work for the realization of something of His King-
    dom in this country.

1983   *Bishop Tutu of South Africa*

I could not be leading a religious life unless I identified myself with the whole of mankind, and that I could not do, unless I took part in politics.

1973   *Mahatma Gandhi*

The Christian meets the world with the Bible in one hand, the daily newspaper in the other.

1980   *Karl Barth*

There are no hopeless situations. There are only men and women who have grown hopeless about them.

1976   *An Old Frenchman after the Battle of Verdum*

I think, as life is action and passion, it is required of a man that he should share the passion and action of his time, or risk the peril of being judged not to have lived.

1972   *Oliver Wendell Holmes, Jr.*

All men on the earth are merely one great family, divided into many branches.

1944   *Bandeau*

To consider mankind otherwise than brethren, to think favors are peculiar to one nation, and exclude others, plainly supposes a darkness in the understanding.

1964   *John Woolman*

Turn therefore away from the despair of the world toward that purer ground where men can stand together to restore the world.

1967   *Dan Wilson*

To the large hearted, the whole world is a friendly home.

1975   *From the Sanskrit*

A friend of man was he, and thus he was a friend of God.

1937   *Wilson Mac Donald*

Religion is the vision of something which stands beyond, behind, and within the passing flux of immediate things.

1958   *Alfred N. Whitehead*

I do dimly perceive that whilst everything around me is ever-changing, ever-dying, there is underlying all that change, a living power that is changeless, that holds all together, that creates, dissolves, and re-creates. That informing power or spirit is God; but since nothing else that I see merely through the senses can or will persist, He alone is...For I can see that in the midst of death, life persists; in the midst of untruth, truth persists; in the midst of darkness, light persists. Hence, I gather that God is Life, Truth, Light. He is Love. He is the supreme Good.

1983   *Mahatma Gandhi*

The life of God sweeps on through the souls of men
in continued revelation and creative newness.

1983   *Thomas Kelly*

Let what ye desire of the universe penetrate you
Let loving kindness and mercy pass through you
And truth be the law of your mouth
For so ye are the channels of the divine sea
Which may not flood the earth, but only steal in
Through rifts in your souls.

1983   *Israel Zangwill*

I am not a God afar off
I am a Brother and a Friend
Within your bosom I reside
And you reside in Me.

1964   *William Blake*

Lord, make me an instrument of Thy peace
Where there is hatred, let me sow love,
Where there is injury, pardon
Where there is doubt, faith
Where there is despair, hope
Where there is darkness, light
And where there is sadness, joy.
O, Divine Master, grant that I may not so much
    seek

        To be consoled as to console
        to be understood as to understand
        to be loved as to love;

For it is in giving that we receive
It is in pardoning that we are pardoned
And it is dying that we are born to eternal life.

1945   *St. Francis of Assisi*

In His will is our peace.

1954   *Dante*

To recompense injury with kindness, this is the law of
 life.

1919   *Lao-Tzu*

With mercy and forbearance shalt thou disarm every
 foe; for want of fuel the fire expires; mercy and
 forbearance bring violence to naught.

1919   *Buddha*

Our work for peace must begin within the private
 world of each one of us.

1963   *Dag Hammarsjöld*

Teach us that we stand daily and wholly in need of
 one another.

1963   *Queen Elizabeth's Prayer Book*

Whenever beauty overwhelms us, whenever wonder silences our chattering hopes and worries, we are close to worship.

1976   *Richard Cabot*

I heard a bird at break of day
Sing from the autumn trees
A song so mystical and calm
So full of certainties.
No man, I think, could listen long
Except upon his knees.
Yet this was but a simple bird
Alone among dead leaves.

1946   *William A. Percy*

This is my Father's world
He shines in all that's fair
In the rustling grass I hear Him pass
He speaks to me everywhere.

1937   *Maltbie Babcock*

I do love my country's good with a respect more tender, more holy, more profound, than mine own
life.

1970   *William Shakespeare*

There is only one light, and I think that is the spirit
within each one of us that will hold out:

> Generosity to the weak
> Magnanimity to the angry and fearful
> And justice for the disadvantaged.

This is the way we will meet our problems in this
country, and in no other way.

1972   *Tom Wicker*

No man has the right to leave the world as he found
it. He must add something to it. Either he must
make its people better or happier, or he must
make the face of the world more beautiful.

1972   *Edward Bok*

Awake at dawn with a winged heart
And give thanks for another day of loving.

1975   *Kahlil Gibran*

Beneath a stormy driven sky
The wind was brisk and keen
And standing there, I needs must pray
Lord, sweep my spirit clean.
Sweep out all trace of greed and pride
Sweep out the seeds of strife
And let me with Thy love express
The joy of bounteous life.

1952   *Richard M. Sutton*

Life is a series of adventures prompted by love.

1973   *The Rev. Henry Sloane Coffin*

A surplus of love is necessary to fill up what is lacking
of love in this world.

1974   *Martin Buber*

The poor deserve not just service and dedication, but
also the joy that belongs to human love.

1984   *Mother Teresa*

O Lord, baptize our hearts into a sense of the conditions and needs of all men.

1974   *George Fox*

Seek love in the pity of others' woes
In the gentle relief of another's care
In the darkness of night and the winter's snow
In the naked and outcast, seek love there.

1967   *William Blake*

Thou shalt love the Lord thy God with all thy heart,
and with all thy soul, and with all thy might. This
is the first and great commandment.
And the second is like unto it: Thou shalt love thy
neighbor as thyself.

1910   *St. Matthew*

Love gives life a purpose and meaning and value.
Love cannot save life from death, but it can fulfill
life's purpose.

1970   *Arnold Toynbee*

Beyond the sea of death love lies
Forever, yesterday, today.

1983   *Christina Rossetti*

God will not send thee into the forest
To hew an oak with a penknife.
If He gives thee a task thou never didst
He will give thee a strength thou never hadst.

1982   *Author Unknown*

One on God's side is a majority.

1931   *Wendell Phillips*

Make my mortal dreams come true
With the work I fain would do
Clothe with life the weak intent
Let me be the thing I meant
Let me find in Thy employ
Peace that dearer is than joy.

1935   *John G. Whittier*

With God, all things are possible.

1938   *St. Matthew*

By one great heart the universe is stirred.

1983   *Margaret Deland*

Religion is not something apart from life and business
Not something for special days or sacred places
It is the whole of life
It is a way of life
It is something that one does and is.

1975   *Rufus M. Jones*

Religion means for me a human being's relation to an
    ultimate reality behind and beyond the phenom-
    ena of the universe in which each of us awakes to
    consciousness.

1975   *Arnold Toynbee*

Our true life lies at a great depth within us.

1984   *Rabindranath Tagore*

Let us give ourselves to God without any reserve, and let us fear nothing. He will love us, and we shall love Him...Even the smallest actions of a simple and common life will be turned to consolation and recompense. We shall meet the approach of death in peace; it will be changed for us into the beginning of the immortal life.

1982   *François de La Mothe Fénelon*

I must confess to a passionate devotion to God...If He be real, and if He be concerned for me, I ask no more. I believe He cares, and that He continues our lives after death, in a fellowship of which we have a foretaste here.

1982   *Thomas R. Kelly*

They that love beyond the world cannot be separated
   by it. Death cannot kill what never dies; nor can
   spirits ever be divided that love and live in the
   same divine principle, the root and record of their
   friendship.

1984   *William Penn*

I shall no longer run from sorrow
Nor seek to avoid him, by going down another street
   of thoughts.
I shall not try to overcome him with my strength;
I shall open the door of my heart to his knock, and
   let him come in.
Whether he be sorrow for my own loss, or for the
   world's pain
I will learn to live with him, steadfast and tender.

1972   *Elizabeth Gray Vining*

God is the final, deepest meaning of all that exists.

1983   *Aldous Huxley*

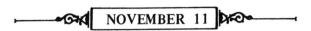

Man's capacity for justice makes democracy possible;
but his inclination to injustice makes democracy
necessary.

1980   *Dr. Reinhold Niebuhr*

To establish these values two centuries ago, a bold
generation of Americans risked their property,
position and life itself. We are their heirs, and
they are sending us a message across the centuries.
The words they made so vivid are now growing
faintly indistinct because they are not heard often
enough. They are words like Justice, Equality,
Unity, Sacrifice, Liberty, Faith, and Love. These
words remind us that the duty of our generation
is to renew our nation's faith - not focussed just
against foreign threats, but against selfishness,
cynicism and apathy.

1980   *Jimmy Carter*

Friendship is the only cement that will ever hold the
world together.

1976   *Woodrow Wilson*

Peace cannot be achieved by force, it can only be
    achieved by understanding.

1983
                                                    Albert Einstein

There shall be peace on earth, but not until
Each child shall daily eat his fill.
Go warmly clad against the winter wind
And learn his lessons with a tranquil mind.
And thus released from hunger, fear and need
Regardless of his color, race or creed
Look upwards, smiling to the skies
His faith in man reflected in his eyes.

1966
                                             Dorothy Roight

No nation lives for itself.
No nation lives but through the service it renders
    to humanity.

1918
                                             Paul Richard

The most urgent item on our agenda in the years immediately ahead is the creation of a world without borders - one which recognizes the common destiny of all mankind.

1976   *Lester R. Brown*

What kind of peace do I mean, and what kind of peace do we ask? Not a Pax Americana enforced in the world by American weapons of war; not the peace of the grave, or the security of the slave... but genuine peace...that makes life on earth worth living - the kind that enables men and nations to grow and hope, and build a better life for their children; not merely peace for Americans, but peace for all men and women; not merely peace in our time, but peace for all time.

1965   *John F. Kennedy*

The best politics is right action.

1956   *Mahatma Gandhi*

This time, like all times, is a very good one, if we but
know what to do with it.

1980   *Ralph W. Emerson*

So, let us be prepared to make mistakes, if we must
make them, on the side of trust, rather than on
the side of mistrust in our fellow men, or in the
peoples around the world. Let us be prepared to
make mistakes on the side of hope, instead of on
the side of despair and fear. So let us go from
here to do the things we can do, and not worry
about what we cannot do.

1974   *Eugene McCarthy*

Lord, we pray not for tranquillity, nor that our trib-
ulations may cease; we pray for Thy spirit and
Thy love, that Thou grant us strength and grace
to overcome adversity.

1966   *Girolamo Savonarola*

God gives us all
Some small sweet way
To set the world rejoicing.

1916   *Author Unknown*

The happiest man is he who learns from Nature the
  lesson of worship.

1937   *Ralph W. Emerson*

Open wide the windows of our spirits
And fill us full of light
Open wide the doors of our hearts
That we may receive and entertain Thee
With all our powers of adoration and love.

1946   *Christina Rossetti*

As food is indispensable for the body, so is prayer indispensable for the soul.

1977   *Mahatma Gandhi*

The time of busyness does not with me differ from the time of prayer, and in the noise and clatter of my kitchen, while several persons are at the same time calling for different things, I possess God in as great tranquility as if I were upon my knees at the Blessed Sacrament.

1978   *Brother Lawrence*

All aspects of life are holy; let us take care not to draw any sharp lines between secular and spiritual life.

1966   *Philadelphia Yearly Meeting of Friends*
1963

The happiness of your life depends upon the quality of your thoughts.

1942

Marcus Aurelius

There needs but thinking right and meaning well; and may this ensure you the soul's calm sunshine, and heartfelt joy.

1966

Abigail Adams

I do not know what your destiny may be, but this I do know:
>   You will always have happiness if you seek
>   and find how to serve.

1963

Dr. Albert Schweitzer to Dr. Tom Dooley

To be a joy-bearer and joy-giver says everything; and if one gives joy to others, one is doing God's work.

1977

Mother Janet Stuart

Sense your power to lift the mood of despair.

1984

Ken Keyes, Jr.

MAN IS A TENDER PLANT

In this our time,
Our sad, new, immeasurably dear time,
Walking at night near the edge, gazing
Down into the abyss, or letting the eyes
Sweep upward, searching out unseen worlds,

It is never enough,
No, never enough now, if you encounter another
Walking the same path, merely to greet him
Carelessly and slip by, eager to begin the descent
To the waiting valley.

Linger with him a moment, ask for news
Of his home, whether he has eaten
Or knows of a place to rest.

Only yesterday
He grew up in prison in the shadow
Of crematoriums for the living,
Last night lay down to sleep
In a city crumbling to dust around him,
Fled from his home to enter a country
Speaking strange tongues,
Hid behind frail doors
From the night-sticks of despair.

Even now it is not certain
Whether he knows the path, or indeed
Will arrive at any haven.

Linger with him, take him by the hand
And bless one another before continuing
On your separate journeys.

Man must be cherished now,
Shielded like a tender plant exposed to too much sun,
Refreshed by the spring waters of caring.

1968   *Winifred Rawlins*

Not without design does God write the music of our
lives.

1984
John Ruskin

If a man constantly aspires, is he not elevated?

1984
Henry D. Thoreau

The greatest thing one man can do for another, is to
confirm the deepest thing within him.

1983
Martin Buber

Man lives by affirmation even more than he does by
bread.

1962
Victor Hugo

If you can accept me as I am, and love me as I am,
then I can change what I am.

1982
Heard in a Friends Meeting

Oh, patient Master Workman of the world
Shaper of all this home of humankind
Teach us the truer trade of making doors
And windows for men's souls -
Windows for letting in love's widening dawn
Doors swinging outward freely on truth's pleasant
    ways
Doors guarding all those helpless ones
Guns cannot guard, nor armies make secure.

1977   *L. Griswold Williams*

Opportunities are not to be neglected; they rarely
    visit us twice.

1953   *Voltaire*

'Tis God gives skill, but not without men's hands. He
    could not make Antonio Stradivari's violins with-
    out Antonio.

1978   *George Eliot*

Lord of all happiness, Lord of all joy
Whose trust, ever child-like, no care could destroy
Be there at our waking, and give us, we pray
Your bliss in our hearts, Lord, at the break of the
      day.

Lord of all eagerness, Lord of all faith
Whose strong hands were skilled at the plane and the
      lathe
Be there at our labor, and give us, we pray
Your strength in our hearts, at the noon of the day.

Lord of all kindliness, Lord of all grace
Your hands swift to welcome, Your arms to embrace
Be there at our homing, and give us, we pray
Your love in our hearts, Lord, at the eve of the day.

Lord of all gentleness, Lord of all calm
Whose voice is contentment, whose presence is balm
Be there at our sleeping, and give us, we pray
Your peace in our hearts, Lord, at the end of the day.

1981   *Jan Struther*

God's goodness hath been great to thee.
Let never day or night unhallowed pass
But still remember what the Lord hath done.

1925   *William Shakespeare*

Let us be thankful upon Thanksgiving Day
Nature is beautiful
Fellow men are dear
Duty is close beside us.
And He is over all.

1953   *The Rev. Phillips Brooks*

Brother and Lord, among thy children sitting
Lord of our toil, bestower of our rest
Lord of our feast, to Thee it is most fitting
Praises and thanks we bring
Our whole heart's best
Jesu, be Thou our guest.

1969   *The Adelynrood Grace*

Now thank we all our God
With hearts and hands and voices
Who wondrous things hath wrought
In whom the world rejoices.

1963   *Martin Rinkert*

Let us praise and thank God in all gladness and
    humility
For all great and simple joys
For the gift of wonder, and the joy of discovery
For the everlasting freshness of experience
For the newness of life each day as we grow older
For the image of Christ in ordinary people
Their forbearance and generosity
Their good temper, their courage and kindness
We thank Thee, O, our Father.

1958   *Author Unknown*

What a man takes in by contemplation, he must
  pour out in love.

1983   *Meister Eckhart*

Thanks for giving me the golden leaf, the red berries
The tiny pine cones, the hard, cold winter wind
That remind me again and again that I am alive.

Who am I to receive such wondrous gifts?
What must I do to deserve such riches?
And the only answer I get is to love
To love Him, to love others, to love myself
To love His whole creation, and to begin to feel
Its vast power, magnificence, love.

1974   *Eloise Quick*

Life begins each morning.

1938   *Leigh Hodges*

Thank God for sleep in the long quiet night
For the clear day calling through the little leaded
    panes,
For the shining well water, and the warm golden
    light
And the paths washed white by singing rains.

For earth's little secret and innumerable ways,
For the carol and the color, Lord, we bring
What things may be of thanks, and that Thou has
    lent our days
Eyes to see and ears to hear, and lips to sing.

1966   *(Abridged, from "Morning Thanksgiving")*
John Drinkwater

Thanksgiving for the past makes us trustful for the
    present, and hopeful for the future.

1983   *Arthur Hall*

O Lord that lends me life
Lend me a heart replete with thankfulness.

1958   *William Shakespeare*

For homely dwelling places
Where childhood's visions linger
For friends and kindly voices
For bread to stay our hunger
And sleep to bring us ease;
For zeal and zest of living
For faith and understanding
For words to tell our loving
For hope of peace unending
We thank, You, Lord, for these.

1982   *Jan Struther*

The Lord bless thee and keep thee
The Lord make His face to shine upon thee
The Lord lift up His countenance upon thee
And give thee peace.

1926   *Numbers 6*

Thou that hast given so much to me
Give one more thing, a grateful heart;
Not thankful when it pleases me
As if Thy blessings had spare days
But such a heart whose pulse
May be Thy praise.

1962   *The Rev. George Herbert*

Thanks be to God, who saves us out of stormy seas
And from dry wilderness;
Who sets our feet upon the rock
Who clarifies and heals our minds
Who opens and expands our hearts
Who steadies and directs our wills
Who fructifies in us delighted joy
In His unending care,
His guiding, and His chastening.

1962   *Anne Forsythe*

Everything is a gift of God, if we know how to make
    use of it.

1961   *Mother Marie des Douleurs*

Oh, thanks be to God for every gift
For beauty spread o'er hill and plain
For summer skies, for winter's drift
Of snowy fleece o'er next year's grain.

1890   *Author Unknown*

Back of the loaf is the snowy flour
And back of the flour is the mill
And back of the mill are the wheat, and the shower
And the sun, and the Father's will.

1956   *Maltbie Babcock*

When thy heart with joy o'erflowing
Sings a thankful prayer
In thy joy, O let thy brother
With thee share.

When thy harvest sheaves ingathered
Fill thy barns with store
To thy God, and to thy brother
Give the more.

1978   *Ethelbert W. Bullinger*

PRAYER FROM SPACE
APOLLO 8

Give us, O God
 The vision which can see
 Thy love in the world
   In spite of human failure.

Give us the faith
 The trust, the goodness
 In spite of our ignorance
  And weakness.

Give us the knowledge
 That we may continue
 To pray with understanding
  Hearts.

And show us
 What each one of us can do
 To set forth the coming
 Of the day of universal
  Peace.
                        Amen

1984   *Frank Borman*

Prayer is not a magical device by which we get what
    we privately want, at the cost of the reliability of
    the natural order, or the common good. Prayer is
    an intellectual discipline in truthfulness and a
    moral discipline in unselfishness. It is the endeavor
    to find out what is true and right, and then to con-
    form to those realities.

1974   *Willard Sperry*

Any meditation or practice of prayer should lead to
    the gaining of strength to remedy the world's
    suffering.

1979   *Damaris Parker-Rhodes*

Jesus did not agonize over motives of service, nor
    attempt to explain the mystery of pain and suf-
    fering. He set about to open men's eyes that they
    might see beauty, to open their ears that they
    might hear truth, to heal the broken-hearted, to
    make the sick whole.
He calls us to do the same.

1969   *Josephine Moffett Benton*

The humble, meek, merciful, just, pious and devout souls are everywhere of one religion; and when death has taken off the mask they will know one another, though the divers liveries they wear here, make them strangers.

1984

William Penn

We are all of us fellow passengers on the same planet, and are all of us equally responsible for the happiness and well-being of the world in which we happen to live.

1982

Hendrik Willem van Loon

In this gentle season
When men remember they are brothers
And know that all children are our children
We urge an end to killing.
Now let it be written
Our nation found a way to peace.

1970

Another Mother for Peace

Human progress never rolls in on the wheels of
    inevitability.

1969   *The Rev. Martin Luther King, Jr.*

Progress is not automatic; the world grows better
    because people wish that it should, and take the
    right steps to make it better.

1969   *Jane Addams*

We pass the word around
We ponder how the case is put by different people
We read the poetry
We meditate over the literature
We play the music
We change our minds
We reach an understanding
Society evolves this way
Not by shouting each other down, but by
the unique capacity of unique individual human
beings to comprehend each other.

1981   *Dr. Lewis Thomas*

rt ye, comfort ye my people", saith yo|
Prepare the way of the Lord, make straig
e desert a highway for our God. Every valle
be exalted, and every mountain and hi
be made low; and the crooked shall be mad
ht and the rough places plain; and the glor
e Lord shall be revealed, and all flesh sha

Isaial

us a Child is born, unto us a Son is given,
he government shall be upon His shoulder;
His name shall be called Wonderful, Counsel-
he Mighty God, the Everlasting Father, the
e of Peace.

Isaiah

mes as we are, that we may become as He is.

William Blake

The American dream is based on the conviction that every individual is of value.

1969   *John W. Gardner*

Man's altruistic and innately co-operative character has brought him along the road to civilization far more than the qualities of the ape and tiger.

1971   *Loren Eiseley*

A clash of doctrines is not a disaster - it is an opportunity.

1962   *Alfred North Whitehead*

There is an immense task incumbent on all men of good will, namely the task of restoring the relations of the human family.

1971   *Pope John XXIII*

You cannot command for yourself the love you would gladly receive...but that noble love, which is not asking, but giving, that you can always have. Wherever your life touches another life, there you have opportunity.

1982   *George S. Merriam*

The whole worth of a kind deed is the love that inspires it.

1982   *The Talmud*

The virtuous deeds of men are not accounted or regarded after our judgment, but after the judgment and good pleasure of God; for God looketh not on the number of works, but to the measure of the love and humility.

1967   *The Little Flowers of St. Francis*

Even in December
The earth will turn
Nearer the sun
Darkness will turn to dawn.
Pause and remember
As the long nights close in
The angels' song, the child
And darkness gone.

1968

Light looked down, and b
"Thither will I go," said L
Peace looked down, and b
"Thither will I go,"' said F
Love looked down, and b
"Thither will I go," said L
So came Light and shone
So came Peace and gave r
So came Love, and broug
And the Word was made
And dwelt among us.

1954

"Comf
    God
    in th
    shall
    shall
    strai
    of th
    see i

1959

For un
    and
    and
    lor, t
    Princ

1961

God bec

1966

We know and feel that we are eternal.

1983   *Benedict de Spinoza*

The true office of any faith is to give life a meaning
    which death cannot destroy.

1984   *Leo Tolstoy*

Do you cherish that of God within you, that His
    power, growing in you may rule your life?

1967   *Book of Discipline, of British Friends*

For God hath not given us the spirit of fear, but of
    power, and of love, and of a sound mind.

1984   *II Timothy*

Whether you understand it or not, God loves you.

1982   *Thomas Merton*

Religion should be a rule of life, not a casual incident in it.

1945   *Benjamin Disraeli*

Build your church within your heart, and take it with you everywhere.

1942   *Author Unknown*

There was a care on my mind, so to pass my time that nothing might hinder me from the most steady attention to the voice of the True Shepherd.

1955   *John Woolman*

They that wait upon the Lord shall renew their strength.

1925   *Isaiah*

A baby is a lovesome thing
And wins our hearts with one accord
And flower of babies was our King
Jesus Christ the Lord.

1969   *Christina Rossetti*

Christmas is a time of promise, the meaning of which
    man has never fully grasped; the joy of it is too
    deep for our small hearts, the message too simple
    and too enormous to be simply believed, except
    by children.

1968   *Jane Tyson Clement*

One laugh of a child will make the holiest day more
    sacred still.

1984   *Robert Ingersoll*

Every child is a holy child.

1982   *Anonymous*

A man's true wealth is the good he does in the world.

1950   *Mohammed*

A clear-sighted eye
A many-sided sympathy
A fine daring, and endless patience
All these are forever necessary for all good living.

1972   *Havelock Ellis*

A friend is one who makes us be our best.

1921   *Ralph W. Emerson*

Christianity has taught us to care
Caring is the Christian thing
Caring is all that matters.

1977   *Baron Friedrich von Hügel*

The aim, if reached or not
Makes great the life.

1975   *Robert Browning*

Let us not pray for a light burden, but for a strong
   back.

1939   *Theodore Roosevelt*

When God closes one door, he usually opens another.

1964   *The Rev. J. D. Jones*

O God, give us grace to accept with serenity the
   things that cannot be changed, courage to change
   the things which should be changed, and the wisdom to know one from the other.

1972   *Dr. Reinhold Niebuhr*

The Lord is my shepherd, I shall not want.

1955   *Psalm 23*

For the love of God is broader
Than the measure of man's mind
And the heart of the Eternal
Is most wonderfully kind.

1955   *The Rev. Frederick Faber*

Nor can we fall below the arms of God
Howsoever low it be we fall.

1958   *William Penn*

And I smile to think God's greatness
Flows around our incompleteness
Round our restlessness, His rest.

1912   *Elizabeth B. Browning*

At this season we move into the dark, the light falters
    as earth tilts toward the void. We wait for the
    coming of One whom we may not recognize.
    Nothing is certain, save that the night shall deep-
    en, and He shall come.

1975   *Rita Rouner*

Jesus, Thou joy of loving hearts
Thou fount of life, Thou light of men
From the best bliss that earth imparts
We turn unfilled to Thee again.

1956   *Bernard of Clairvaux*

O come, desire of nations, bind
In one the hearts of all mankind
Bid Thou our sad divisions cease
And be Thyself our King of Peace.

1978   *Based on a Latin Hymn, 9th Century*

The world needs a change in outlook, from fear to faith, based on the kind of love that Jesus taught; from compulsion with its trust in weapons, to co-operation, based on the dignity and worth of the human person.

1952   *Philadelphia Yearly Meeting of Friends*

Peace is a shelter for all that we love
   It is the only house in which men can now live
Peace is love conquering fear; it is a lively concern for
    all men
     For friend and for rival, for the lovely earth, for
     life and for joy
Peace is world order, and political institutions
    It is justice and the control over the strong
    It is mercy, and the restraint over the merciless.

1973   *Kenneth Boulding*
                                              (abridged)

May Thy truth unite all mankind into one brother-hood. May our love for one another be our crown of glory and armor of strength.

1961   *From a Hebrew Prayer*

No heaven can come to us unless we find rest in
to-day.
No peace lies in the future, which is not hidden in
this precious little instant.
There is radiance and glory in the darkness, could
we but see.

1943   *Fra Giovanni (1513)*

In the morning, fix your purpose.

1899   *Author Unknown*

Grant unto us, O Lord, the royalty of inward happiness, and the serenity which comes from living
close to Thee. Daily renew in us the sense of joy,
and let Thy eternal spirit dwell in our souls and
bodies, filling every corner with light and gladness; so that, bearing about with us the infection
of a good courage, we may be diffusers of life, and
meet all that comes, of good or ill, even death
itself, with gallant and high-hearted happiness;
giving Thee thanks always for all things.

1956   *L. H. M. Soulsby*

The great man is he who does not lose his child's heart.

1937   *Mencius (372-289 B.C.)*

Teach us delight in simple things.

1949   *Rudyard Kipling*

The gloom of the world is but a shadow. Behind it, yet within reach, is joy.

1955   *Fra Giovanni*

Above the cloud with its shadow is the star with its light.

1969   *Victor Hugo*

Wondrous is the strength of cheerfulness.

1923   *Thomas Carlyle*

I need wide spaces in my heart
Where faith and I can go apart
And grow serene.
Life gets so choked by busy living
Kindness, so lost in fussy giving
That love slips by unseen.

1938   *L. R. B.*

Go placidly amidst the noise and haste, and remem-
    ber what peace there may be in silence.

1968   *Desiderata*

Life from the Center is a life of unhurried peace and
    power.
It is simple, it is serene.
It is amazing; it is triumphant; it is radiant
It takes no time, but it occupies all our time.
And it makes our life program new and overcoming
We need not get frantic
He is at the helm.

1981   *Thomas Kelly*

New every year, newborn and newly dear
He comes with tidings and a song
The ages long, the ages long.

1965   *Alice Meynell*

Thou shalt know Him when He comes, not by any
    din of drums
Nor the vantage of His airs, nor by anything He wears
Neither by His crown, nor His gown
But His presence known shall be
By the holy harmony
That His coming makes in thee.

1959   *Unknown 15th Century Writer*

May the love that led the wise men to Bethlehem's
    open door, enter your heart, and abide with you.

1943   *Author Unknown*

Tell me, how may I join in this holy feast
With all the kneeling world and I of all, the least
Fear not, O faithful heart, but bring what most is
    meet
Bring love alone, true love alone, and lay it at His
    feet.

1962   *Richard Watson Gilder*

The feet of the humblest may walk in the field
Where the feet of the holiest trod
'Tis then, is the marvel to mortals revealed
When the silvery trumpets of Christmas have pealed
That mankind are the children of God.

1964   *The Rev. Phillips Brooks*

Whenever visions of the light
Disturb the sleeping souls of men
Night trails away its shadowy flight
And Christ is born again.

1964   *14th Century Monk*

The whole world is my family.

1983   *Pope John XXIII*

A friend is one who walks in when the rest of the
world walks out.

1928   *Author Unknown*

Start looking for what is valid in every man.

1971   *Albert Camus*

Behave toward everyone as if receiving a great guest.

1982   *Confucius*

O, God, make the door of this house wide enough to
receive all who need human love and fellowship,
narrow enough to shut out all envy, pride and
strife.
God, make the door of this house the gateway to
Thine eternal Kingdom.

1978   *On the door of St. Stephen's in London*

Blessed is he that considereth the poor.

1904   *Psalm 41*

A single example of hunger is one too many.

1978   *Arthur Simon*

Have you bettered the poor man's narrow span?
Have you brightened the way he trod?
Perchance when he learns the love of man
He may trust the love of God.

1907   *Author Unknown*

Give what you have; to some it may be better than
   you dare to think.

1906   *Henry W. Longfellow*

Who gives himself with his alms feeds three
Himself, his hungering neighbor, and Me.

1886   *James R. Lowell*

In the faces of men and women, I see God.

1982   *Walt Whitman*

We can be so overwhelmed by the extent of the
    world's problems that the obvious need before us
    can be missed. For most of us, it is in the minute
    particular that we give ourselves to the eternal
    order of things: in our own living rooms, in our
    own streets, in the way we live, and love, and care,
    minute by minute; in the chance encounters of
    every day, as well as in the planned work which
    we do.

1983   *Dorothy Steere*

The heart grows rich in giving.

1901   *Author Unknown*

Consecrate with Thy presence the way our feet may
    go, and the humblest work will shine, and the
    roughest place be made plain.

1968   *The Rev. James Martineau*

This little child of holy birth
Shall be the joy of all the earth.

1917   *Martin Luther*

On high tonight the stars are spread
Self same as when they sifted down
Their beams upon the manger bed
In Judah's town!
But here on earth so much of change
Such groping and so many fears
So much forgetting the far range
Of healing years.
Unchanging firmament above
Serene despite our disarray
And close, so close, unchanging love
To light the way.

1949   *Leigh Hodges*

How shall we love Thee, holy hidden being
If we love not the world which Thou has made.
O, give us brother love for better seeing
Thy Word made flesh and in a manger laid.
Thy Kingdom come, O Lord, Thy will be done!

1916   *Laurence Housman*

To acknowledge and confirm the personal value and
    dignity of each one of our fellow men would per-
    haps be the most real and significant Christmas
    present that mankind could make to the world.

1981   *Staff of Foyer Unitas, Rome*

Rise, and bake your Christmas bread
Christians, rise! the world is bare
And blank and dark, with want and and care
Yet Christmas comes in the morning!

Rise, and light your Christmas fire
Christians, rise! the world is old
And time is weary and worn and cold
Yet Christmas comes in the morning!

Rise and open wide the door
Christians, rise! the world is wide
And many there are that stand outside
Yet Christmas comes in the morning.

1972   *Dora Greenwell*

A great and mighty wonder to-day on earth is done
To God on high be glory, and peace on earth to men!

1978   *St. Germanus*

What can I give Him, poor as I am?
If I were a shepherd, I would bring a lamb
If I were a wise man, I would do my part
Yet what can I give Him? Give Him my heart!

1972   *Christina Rossetti*

I place these gifts on my altar this Christmas
Gifts that are mine, as the years are mine:
The quiet hopes that flood the earnest cargo of my
    dreams
The best of all good things for those I love
A fresh new trust for all whose faith is dim
The love of life, God's precious gift, in reach of all
Seeing in each day the seeds of the morrow
Finding in each struggle the strength of renewal
Seeing in each person the face of my brother.
I place these gifts on my altar this Christmas
Gifts that are mine, as the years are mine.

1980   *The Rev. Howard Thurman*

Ask why a belief in a cosmic power is tied into the birth of a child in poverty. You may find in the answer a place to steady yourself, as the waves of change sweep by.

1967   *The Rt. Rev. Paul Moore, Jr.*

Christ is the coming of God in and through the process of history - God revealed to us in the persuasive terms of personal life and loving will.

1958   *Rufus M. Jones*

There is no compulsion in God's dealings with man, but persuasion and infinite love.

1887   *Author Unknown*

Are you willing to believe that love is the strongest thing in the world, and that the blessed life which began in Bethlehem nineteen hundred years ago is the image and brightness of Eternal Love? Then you can keep Christmas, and if you can keep it for a day, why not always?

1957   *The Rev. Henry van Dyke*

All creatures sing around us, and we sing
We bring our own selves as our offering
Our very selves we render to our King.

1984   *Christina Rossetti*

When the star in the sky is gone
When the kings and princes are home
When the shepherds are back with their flocks
The work of Christmas begins:
To find the lost
To heal the broken
To feed the hungry
To release the prisoners
To rebuild the nations
To bring peace among brothers.

1984   *The Rev. Howard Thurman*

It is Christmas every day that we love our fellow men.
  If we take them into our hearts, if we go toward
  them with love, at that moment Christ is born.

1962   *Père Journet*

DECEMBER 28

And who is thy neighbor?
Any man whose need of thee lays claim
Friend and foe alike
Thou must not make division
Thy mind, heart, soul and strength must ever search
To find the road to all men's need of thee
This is the highway of the Lord.

1975   *The Rev. Howard Thurman*

God is seated in the hearts of all.

1921   *The Bhagavad-Gita*

The nearest way to God is through love's open door.

1971   *Angelus Silesius*

Dear Lord, who sought at dawn of day
The solitary woods to pray
In quietness we come to ask
Thy presence for the daily task.

1936   *Harry Webb Farrington*

More things are wrought by prayer
Than this world dreams of.

1890   *Alfred, Lord Tennyson*

In the silent hours of the morning I view Thee.
In the daytime whilst I am working, Thou art with
    me.
In the night when I am resting Thou loveth and
    beholdeth me.

1957   *(From a Nepalese Prayer Wheel)*

Silence is not the absence of the world, but the pres-
    ence of God.

1963   *Spes Sancta*

God, who a thousand years doth wait
To work a thousandth part of Thy great plan
In me create a humble, patient heart.

1978   *George MacDonald*

He is the living God to save
My rock while sorrow's toils endure
My banner and my stronghold sure
The cup of life whene'er I crave.
I place my soul within His palm
Before I sleep as when I wake
And though my body I forsake
Rest in the Lord in fearless calm.

1970   *Jewish Hymn*

O may this bounteous God
Through all our life be near us
With ever joyful hearts
And blessed peace to cheer us.
And keep us in His grace
And guide us when perplexed
And free us from all ills
In this world and the next.

1930   *The Rev. Martin Rinkert*

Ring out, wild bells, to the wild sky
The flying cloud, the frosty light
The year is dying in the night
Ring out, wild bells, and let him die!

Ring out the old, ring in the new
Ring, happy bells. across the snow
The year is going, let him go
Ring out the false, ring in the true.

Ring out the shapes of foul disease
Ring out the narrowing lust of gold
Ring out the thousand wars of old
Ring in the thousand years of peace.

Ring in the valiant man and free
The larger heart, the kindlier hand
Ring out the darkness of the land
Ring in the Christ that is to be!

1903   *Alfred, Lord Tennyson (abridged)*

The best of all is, God is with us!

1974   *The Rev. John Wesley*

ACKNOWLEDGMENTS

Grateful acknowledgment is made to the following authors or their representatives, for permission to include selections from their writings or speeches:

AMERICAN FRIENDS SERVICE COMMITTEE; JAMES BALDWIN; COLIN BELL; LEONARD BERNSTEIN and STEPHEN SCHWARTZ for lines from *Mass,*© 1971; FRANK BORMAN for "Prayer from Space -- Apollo 8": KENNETH BOULDING for selections from *Sonnets from the Interior Life, and Other Autobiographical Verse, The Nayler Sonnets,* and *The Meaning of the Twentieth Century.*

THE REV. A. BURNS CHALMERS for lines from a sermon by THE REV. ANDREW B. CHALMERS; JONATHAN DODD, of Dodd, Mead & Co., and DR. ROBERT GIBBS, and DEAN PETER KEPROS of the University of New Brunswick (Canada), for their help in locating sources of the lines of BLISS CARMAN; STEPHEN G. GARY; CESAR CHAVEZ; THE REV. WILLIAM COFFIN; NORMAN COUSINS for lines from *Human Options;* THE REV. ARTHUR FOOTE, for an excerpt from *Taking Down the Defenses;* BLISS FORBUSH; ANNE FORSYTHE; and CHRISTOPHER FRY, for lines from *The Firstborn,* and *A Sleep of Prisoners.*

JOHN GARDNER, for a excerpt from *No Easy Victories;* ELIZABETH GOUDGE; LOUISE H. SCLOVE, for lines from *Death and General Putnam,* by ARTHUR GUITERMAN; THE REV. THEODORE HESBURGH; MARY HOXIE JONES for a stanza from her poem "Even in December", *in Beyond This Stone,* and for her permission to quote from the writings of RUFUS M. JONES; also to THE RUFUS JONES TRUST for their permission for the latter; RICHARD M. KELLY for excerpts from *A Testament of Devotion,* by THOMAS R. KELLY; MARGARETHE LACHMUND, for lines from *Thine Adversary on the Way* and to FLORENCE KITE, translator; MADELEINE L'ENGLE; SYLVIA LOTSPEICH, for a quotation from WILLIAM LOTSPEICH; NORMAN MAILER; THE RT. REV. PAUL MOORE, JR.; MOTHER TERESA, and THE MISSION-ARIES OF CHARITY for a selection from MOTHER TERESA; DR. URSULA NIEBUHR for an excerpt from her book *Justice and Mercy,* for a line from DR. REINHOLD NIEBUHR'S book *The Children of Light and The Children of Darkness,* and for the "Serenity" prayer; WINIFRED RAWLINS for lines from *Fire Within,* and her poem "Man is a Tender Plant"; DAVID RICHIE; TESSA SAYLE for permission to use four lines from *Immanence,* by EVELYN

UNDERHILL; HENRY SCATTERGOOD; THOMAS SCATTER-GOOD; EDMUND SPAETH, JR.; ELIZABETH STEVENS for two quotations from LEWIS STEVENS; LEWIS THOMAS; THE HOWARD THURMAN EDUCATIONAL TRUST for excerpts from the following books by HOWARD THURMAN: *Disciplines of the Spirit*, *Meditations of the Heart*, and *The Mood of Christmas*; ELIZABETH VINING; ELIE WIESEL; GERALD WEISS; TOM WICKER; MRS. HARRISON YOUNG, and THE SOCIETY OF THE COMPANIONS OF THE HOLY CROSS, for the Adelynrood Grace; and OLIVER ZANGWILL for lines from "Jehovah", by ISRAEL ZANGWILL.

Grateful acknowledgment is made also to the publishers and copywriter owners listed below for the permission they have given to reprint the following selections:

GEORGE ALLEN AND UNWIN, LTD., for a selection by SIR OLIVER LODGE, from *Inner Light*, M. C. ALBRIGHT et al. Eds. 1931.

BOARD OF CHRISTIAN EDUCATION OF THE PRESBYTERIAN CHURCH IN THE U.S.A., for lines from *The Book of Common Worship*, © 1946, renewed 1974.

JONATHAN CAPE, LTD., and EXECUTORS OF THE LAURENCE HOUSMAN ESTATE, for the poem "Light Looked Down", from *The Little Plays of St. Francis*, v. 2, and for additional lines from *The Collected Poems of Laurence Housman*.

CHRISTIAN LITERATURE CRUSADE, INC., of Fort Washington, Pa., and THE SOCIETY FOR PROMOTING CHRISTIAN KNOWLEDGE, London, for the lines from *Toward Jerusalem*, by Amy Carmichael.

THE CHRISTOPHERS, for two passages from their publications.

CONTEMPORARY BOOKS, INC., for lines reprinted from *Collected Verse* of EDGAR A. GUEST,© 1934 by Contemporary Books, Inc.

DODD, MEAD & CO., for lines selected from "Daisies", from BLISS CARMAN'S *Poems*.

DOUBLEDAY & CO., INC., for the excerpt from "Outwitted", from *The Shoes of Happiness*, by EDWIN MARKHAM, © 1915, Doubleday.

EVANGELICAL PUBLISHERS, for the poem "God Hath Not

Promised", from *Songs of Faith and Comfort*, by ANNIE J. FLINT.

FAMILY SERVICE AMERICA for lines excerpted from "A Social Worker's Creed", by LINTON B. SWIFT, © 1946 Family Service America.

GOLDEN QUILL PRESS, for permission to quote a stanza from "Even in December", from *Beyond This Stone*, by MARY HOXIE JONES, © Golden Quill Press, 1965; also for the poem "Do Not Go Wrathfully", from *Fire Within*, by WINIFRED RAWLINS, © Golden Quill Press 1959, and for her poem "Man is a Tender Plant", © Golden Quill Press 1969.

HARCOURT BRACE JAVANOVICH INC., for a passage from *Hour of Gold, Hour of Lead*, by ANNE MORROW LINDBERGH, © 1973, by Anne Morrow Lindbergh.

HARPER AND ROW PUBLISHERS, INC., for selections from *A Testament of Devotion*, by THOMAS R. KELLY, ©1941 Harper and Row, renewed 1969 by Lois Lael Kelly Stabler; also for an excerpt from *No Easy Victories*, by JOHN W. GARDNER © 1968, by the author.

HODDER AND STOUGHTON, LTD., and ANTHONY SHEIL ASSOCIATES, LTD., for an excerpt from "God Knows", from *The Gate of the Year*, by MINNIE L. HASKINS, © 1940.

HOLT, RINEHART AND WINSTON, INC., for three quotations from *My Life with Martin Luther King, Jr.*, by CORETTA SCOTT KING, © 1969, by the author.

ALFRED A. KNOPF, INC., for excerpts from *The Prophet*, by KAHLIL GIBRAN, © 1923; also for lines from The *Dream Keeper and Other Poems*, by LANGSTON HUGHES, © 1932; also for selections from *Markings*, by Dag HAMMARSKJÖLD, translated by LEIF SJOBERG, and W.H.AUDEN, © 1964; for the poem "Overtones", from *The Collected Poems of WILLIAM PERCY*, © 1920, 1943, by LeRoy Pratt Percy.

MACMILLAN PUBLISHING CO., INC., for the line from "The Pity of Love", from *The Poems of W.B. YEATS*, R. FINNERAN, Ed. © 1983; also for excerpts from the following works of SIR RABINDRANATH TAGORE: *Gitanjali, Fruit-Gathering* and *Stray Birds*, found in *Collected Poems and Plays*, c© 1916, by MacMillan Publishing Co., renewed 1944 by R. Tagore; also for a selection from *Easter* by JOHN MASEFIELD, © 1929, by the publisher, renewed 1957 by the Author. Also for lines from "The Seekers", from *Poems* © 1912, by the publisher, renewed 1940 by John Masefield.

McGRAW HILL BOOK CO., for lines from "The Children's Charter", by DOROTHY ROIGHT, in *Ride with the Sun*, HAROLD COURLANDER, Ed©1955.

METHUEN & CO., for a stanza from The *Selected Poems of JOHN OXENHAM*, CHARLES L. WALLIS, Ed.©1948.

MOREHOUSE-BARLOW, INC., for permission to reprint the poem "I Sing a Song of the Saints of God", by LESBIA SCOTT, from *The Hymnal,* of the Protestant Episcopal Church in America.

NAVAJIVAN TRUST, Ahmedabad, India, for selections from The *Wit and Wisdom of GANDHI*, H. Jack, Ed. © 1951, by the Beacon Press; and for selections from other writings of Mahatma Gandhi.

W. W. NORTON, CO., INC., for two excerpts from *Human Options,* by NORMAN COUSINS, © 1981, by the author.

OXFORD UNIVERSITY PRESS for the poem "Lord of all Hopefulness, Lord of all Joy", and a stanza from "We Thank You, Lord of Heaven", by JAN STRUTHER, found in *Enlarged Songs of Praise;* for a stanza of "Father Eternal, Ruler of Creation", by LAURENCE HOUSMAN, also in *Enlarged Songs of Praise;* for a verse from *Piae Cantiones,* "Spring Has Now Unwrapped the Flowers", Tr. P. DEARMER, in *The Oxford Book of Carols;* for a passage from CHRISTOPHER FRY'S *A Sleep of Prisoners,* © 1951, and one from *The Firstborn,*©1964; and a prayer "O Thou Who Makest the Stars", from *Divine Service,* by W. E. ORCHARD, 1921.

PENDLE HILL PUBLICATIONS for an excerpt from *Thine Adversary on the Way,* by MARGARETHE LACHMUND, tr. by FLORENCE KITE, © 1979.

G. SCHIRMER, INC., and AMBERSON ENTERPRISES, INC., for an excerpt from *Mass,* by LEONARD BERNSTEIN and STEPHEN SCHWARTZ © 1971 by the authors.

CHARLES SCRIBNER'S SONS, for lines from A *Diary of Private Prayer,* by JOHN BAILLIE, © 1949, Charles Scribner's Sons, renewed 1977 by Jan Fowler Baillie; for lines from *The Tribe of the Helpers,* from *Chosen Poems,* by HENRY VAN DYKE, © 1927 Charles Scribner's Sons, renewed 1955, Tertius Van Dyke; also lines from "God of the Open Air" from "Hymn of Joy", and from "The Toiling of Felix", all also found in *Chosen Poems,* by Henry Van Dyke; also for a line from *The Children of Light and the Children of Darkness,* by REINHOLD

NIEBUHR © 1944, Charles Scribner's Sons; renewed 1972 by Ursula Keppel-Compton Niebuhr; new foreword © 1960 Reinhold Niebuhr.

SELF REALIZATION FELLOWSHIP, for selections from *Metaphysical Meditations,* by PARMAHANSA YOGANANDA © 1964.

SIDGWICK & JACKSON, LTD., for the poem "Morning Thanksgiving", from *Poems 1908 - 1914,* by JOHN DRINK-WATER; and for four lines from "The Flying Wheel", by KATHARINE TYNAN HINKSON..

SIERRA CLUB BOOKS for two excerpts from *This is the American Earth,* by ANSEL ADAMS and NANCY NEWHALL, © 1960 Sierra Club.

THE UNITARIAN-UNIVERSALIST SERVICE COMMITTEE, for a poem.

THE YOUNG MEN'S CHRISTIAN ASSOCIATION for the poem "He Sang at His Bench in Nazareth", by LESLIE S. CLARK; also for two poems by S. RALPH HARLOW: "Who is so Low", and "Create in Us the Splendor"

THE YOUNG WOMEN'S CHRISTIAN ASSOCIATION NATIONAL BOARD, for a prayer by L.H.M.SOULSBY, in *Prayers for a Busy Day* © 1938.

A diligent effort has been made to locate the original sources of the quotations chosen from the century of calendars, and to secure permission for their use. Any errors or omissions will be rectified in future editions of this book, upon notification to the compiler.